CLEAN AT 15

CLEAN AT 15

ANYONE, FROM ANYWHERE, CAN GET CLEAN ANYTIME

RYAN BOYD

The author has tried to recreate events, locations, and conversations from his memories of them. The author has made every effort to give credit to the source of any images, quotes, or other material contained within and obtain permissions when feasible.

This book is not intended to replace the need for therapy or counseling. Opinions in this book are provided for information purposes only and are not intended as a substitute for the therapeutic advice of a competent and knowledgeable counselor or psychologist/psychiatrist. The reader should always consult a trusted counselor or doctor in matters relating to his/her health and particularly with respect to any condition that may require immediate medical attention. The information provided in this book should not be construed as personal medical advice or instruction. Self-diagnosis and self-treatment are not recommended and may indeed be dangerous. Readers who fail to consult competent, trusted therapists assume the risk of any injuries or illness.

Copyright © 2021 by Ryan Boyd

All rights reserved. No part of this book may be reproduced or transmitted in any form or by any means, electronic or mechanical, including photocopying, recording, or any information storage and retrieval system, without permission in writing from the author.

ISBN: 978-0-578-88857-6

Printed in the United States of America   040521

⊚This paper meets the requirements of ANSI/NISO Z39.48-1992 (Permanence of Paper)

For all those who struggle with addiction or know someone who has—past and present.

And . . . To Susan.

CONTENTS

Preface	ix
Introduction	xi

Chapter One
    Early Childhood: 0–10 Years Old   1

Chapter Two
    My Second Decade (First Half):
    11–15 Years Old   15

Chapter Three
    Getting Clean: 8/14/97 (My Clean Date),
    15 Years Old   27

Chapter Four
    Twelve-Step Recovery   37

Chapter Five
    Teens: 15–18 Years Old (1–3 Years Clean)   41

Chapter Six
    College: 19–22 Years Old (4–7 Years Clean)   51

Chapter Seven
    Graduation & Japan: 23–25 Years Old
    (8–10 Years Clean)   61

Chapter Eight
    48 States in 48 Days: 26–28 Years Old
    (10–13 Years Clean)   73

Chapter Nine
    Athens, GA: 29–31 Years Old
    (14–16 Years Clean)   87

Chapter Ten
    Austin, TX: 32–34 Years Old
    (17–19 Years Clean)   95

Chapter Eleven
    Losing Everything: 35–37 Years Old
    (20–22 Years Clean)   107

Chapter Twelve
    In Closing   117

Acknowledgments   121

PREFACE

I went to my first rehab at twelve years old, just after I started doing drugs. Even though I disliked the feeling of being high, I kept using. I used drugs that I said I would never use. I thought about suicide every day and stuck a shotgun in my mouth at thirteen, but couldn't pull the trigger. I was a convicted felon at fifteen and hated my life. I used for about two and a half years in all. I stopped while I was in rehab for the third time, and I still felt miserable. I needed an answer. I was introduced to a twelve-step fellowship again in that rehab. I'd grown tired of living in, and creating more, pain. I wanted relief. We read from a text about recovery (written by addicts for addicts), and this time I believed it. I started feeling that I was on a path that could lead me out of my pain. The day I left treatment I went directly to a meeting. They told me they loved me and that they wanted me to keep coming back. And I did.

INTRODUCTION

It's January 1, 2020. If you're reading this book, we've all made it into another decade. I would like to tell you, the reader, something from the start, on the first page of this book.

I love you.

I may not know you, but I love you. You will not be unloved from this moment on, and you were always loved. Someone somewhere has always loved you. No matter what. No matter what you have done. I'll say it once more—I love you—and I'm not the only one. Don't ever forget that, people love you!

When you find yourself from time to time wondering who cares about you, a good thing to do is replay their faces in your mind, words that you have exchanged, or your experiences with those that love you. Also, there is an exercise I have found to be very eye-opening.

EXERCISE

If you take a pen and paper, and write down all the names you can think of, of all the people that love you or know you, there may be dozens, or hopefully hundreds, of people that come across the page that love you or have loved you. You will hopefully realize that you are loved and have been loved. Do this exercise if, and whenever you're, in doubt, either on paper or in your mind, if you are ever wondering if anyone cares about you.

If you do not feel loved by others, or have never felt loved by others, don't worry, someone right here loves you! I do! Someone always has loved you and always will love you; it just may take some time to figure out who those people are.

This is a book written by an addict for addicts, and for anyone who would like to step into the mind of an addict and possibly view what it is like to experience life as an addict from an onlooker's perspective. Only addicts can experience what it is like to be an addict, and our understanding of each other as addicts, our deep empathy for each other, is unparalleled and cannot be fully experienced by nonaddicts.

I am telling my story in this book, the only one that I know. I may draw heavily from the experiences of other addicts and from the books that I have read, the theories and explanations that lie in my mind, and I am coming from a point of intention that will hopefully make the world a better place.

I have combined my thoughts and my memories in the following pages into an all-in-one inclusive format in which I tell you parts of my story in chronological order. I will explain how I felt about certain events that took place in my life then, how I feel about those events now, and the thoughts and maybe the questions that the events in my life brought up then or still bring up now. I truly hope this book inspires those that read it, and most importantly, I hope that this book helps someone or many to not die from the horrors of active addiction or from the pain experienced in life while in recovery.

I almost died using, I almost died clean, and this is my story.

CHAPTER ONE

EARLY CHILDHOOD: 0–10 YEARS OLD

The first memory that I have is being in a car, in the parking lot of a grocery store. My father was buckling me in, or maybe unbuckling me to take me out of the car. I remember his face. It's a blurry image, but it still exists in my mind. I also remember the color of the car's interior. I think it was red . . .

The next few years of my life were some of the worst years of my life, and they set the pace and pain from there on. I feel I may never get over some of what happened, just better with it on the inside. It is my hope in telling you the following (what happened) that my pain is lessened, and that yours may be lessened as well.

WARNING: This may hurt. The following incidents that I will be telling you about that happened to me from the ages of three to ten years old may bring up some pain for you. Stay close to those that love you and your support network while reading this book if you are easily affected by the painful events of others or if this book brings up pain that you may need to process. DO NOT FEEL ALL YOUR PAIN ALONE.

When I was three years old, we were living in a town in Southern Oregon. A beautiful sunlit town, a small town, a place where kids could walk around, walk to and from school, just a real nice place. I remember tying my shoes for the first time, roaming the hills behind the house to the not-so-distant crater that was one of the most amazing things I had ever seen. I remember having my tonsils taken out before that when I was two years old in Portland, Oregon. Specifically, I remember the nurses and the care that I was given. I would ask nicely for a popsicle and the nurses would bring me one. My older sister (I have two older sisters) had her tonsils taken out too. We were both in the hospital together. I remember listening to a Michael Jackson cassette tape on a Walkman when I had chicken pox and had to lie in bed.

There is a memory that has stayed in my mind since then. Around that time, when I was three, my mother, Susan had married a man named Dan. He was apparently a churchgoer, or member of one of the local churches, a drug user (possibly an addict), and I know nothing of his history other than that. Those two things are all I know about the man that stabbed my mother in front of me when I was three.

It was a sunny day. I remember being in the yard with my sisters. We were not allowed to be in the house that day; we were afraid because our stepfather, the only father we had really ever known, was in the house beating our mother. We could hear her screaming. I felt like my sisters and I were like scared dogs stuck in the backyard, trying desperately to help a human inside because they were being hurt, but we couldn't get inside. There was nothing we could do.

Then, one of us, my older sister or myself, decided to go inside to help our mother. I remember seeing my older sister's face, her crying, I was crying, we were all crying. We were all scared. I went in.

I saw Dan on top of my mom on the floor in their bedroom, and he was holding her down. There was a pocketknife on the nightstand, and I remember seeing him grab the knife. Then I can't see anything past that in my memories.

My mother was in and out of the hospital for the next year, or more, maybe. I don't remember. I do not remember who took care of us, what we did, or why she stayed with him after that. Yes, she stayed with Dan after he stabbed her. There are three houses in my memory: a sunlit-backyard house (where she was stabbed), a small white house where I was beaten with a belt by Dan (he may have broken my back, and I later had to have surgery on my back at the age of thirty-six), and a big gray house that hugged the hills.

In the house where he may have broken my back, I remember the day, the room, and how he did it. He told me to stand at the foot of the bed then he locked the door and began to beat me with a belt. My mother may have tried to get him to stop (I vaguely remember if she did or not).

In the house that hugged the hills, I remember peering into my mother's stab wound as it was healing while she was lying on the couch.

In every house we lived in with Dan, he beat my sisters, he beat me, and he not only beat my mother, but almost killed her. He spanked me one time and told me that he spanked me because "he loved me." My mother later told me that she thought that he was high when he beat us. It makes sense. Whether a man or woman is high or drunk, they are not their true human self and are capable of some pretty inhuman things, i.e. beating each other, saying hurtful things, or killing themselves or killing or hurting others. Humans can be horrible to each other. Chemicals in a human can make a bad situation worse.

Something in my mother probably left or was taken by Dan. I know that her life was almost taken by him, but what else? What else did he take from her? Her dignity, self-respect, humility, her humanness, her ability to love and be loved? I will never know what he took from her. I watched my mother struggle for the next twenty-seven years of her life, from the time I was three years old till the time she died. I watched her lose herself and her ability or will to live, countless times. I only know what I saw her do after Dan, not completely how he affected her. Although I forgive him, he was, and is, one of the worst humans I have ever came across, and I am reminded almost daily, sometimes in my conscious mind, and probably always in my subconscious mind, of what not to do that Dan did in fact do.

I've learned that the addict or nonaddict is really only capable of four things: hurting themselves, hurting others, using (chemicals, each other, food, sex, money, power, etc.), or finding positive solutions. A positive solution is one in which hurting yourself, hurting another, or using is not an option.

Back to Dan. I forgive the man. I forgive the men and women that have ever hurt themselves or someone else in any way. I believe, as my sponsor tells me, that "forgiveness is not for them, it's for you." I also believe in the power of knowing that you yourself are forgiven by another. I believe that if I forgive you, right now, you will be set free in some way—from all you have done, from all that has happened to you, from all you think you have done.

I FORGIVE YOU.

You are worthy of love and respect. You are human. We are not always capable of seeing the truth. Sometimes, it is not until the smoke clears or the dust settles—or, in the case of the addict that uses the twelve steps, and a good inventory—that we are able to see our part in some situations, or if we had any part at all in those situations.

My friend Paul says, "Every truth is but a half-truth." This I would agree with, only adding to it the fact that if there are two people involved in a situation, both competent with fully functional memories, there may be a difference in the minds of both people of how a situation went down. Otherwise, the truth as we know it may be subject to change. Five people could have witnessed the same event and all five people may have developed a different truth from the other regarding the event.

We are not always capable of seeing the truth. The truth in general, the truth for ourselves, the truth of another—the truth is not always certain. One thing that I am certain of and that is permanently in my mind: the truth is Dan stabbed my mother and beat my sisters and I. Dan once ripped the earrings out of my mother's ears. He was truthfully sick, truthfully ill in some way, whether it was mental, emotional, or spiritual (or all three). He was so sick that he endangered the lives of a mother and her three small children, as well as marked pain upon them for the rest of their lives. It has been up to my mother (till the day she died when I was thirty years old), my two sisters, and I to deal with the pain he inflicted upon us, not only physically, but mentally and emotionally. And what spirituality or God exists when there are men like Dan, or to the far extreme, men like Hitler, roaming the earth, killing and doing the worst evil that humans are capable of?

In order to deal with having Dan in my life and being able to experience some sort of spirituality (which I have always equated to not just a connection with a power greater than myself, but also a connection to reality), I can recall my sponsor telling me the story of when a member of clergy visited a field of carnage, otherwise known as a battlefield. The member of clergy (minister or priest) was asked a harrowing question by one of the officers. The question goes something like this: "How can God allow something like this to happen?" The clergyman simply replied, "God didn't do this, man did."

I do not believe that God allows horrible and unspeakable things to happen. I do believe that mankind and womankind can be absolutely pure evil to each other, and that God is not the reason why something extremely heinous happens. I am going to cue you in and tell you that one of the biggest reasons why I have been able to get better with Dan, and forgive him, is because my Higher Power, or God (Good Orderly Direction, Group of Druggies, Great Out Doors), that I believe in is only love—humans are only love at the core and are unfortunately capable of great wrongdoing to each other.

If God is only love, then how could Dans or Hitlers of the world exist?

For me the answer is simple: God does not control humans.

A God is merely, or can be, if believed in by an individual, a source of nonhuman strength and love. That is my personal belief on God and why bad things happen in a world where God is supposedly in charge. This is a very deep, involved, and personal belief for me and helps me to stay alive and stay clean. I do not expect anyone to adapt my beliefs for themselves or share them with me. In twelve-step recovery, we are allowed to choose the God of our own understanding, and in fact, there may be as many understandings of God on earth as there are people that have a belief in one or more!

Choose your own power. One that is love and wants the best for you. I would not have survived to this point in my life without the belief in something that helps guide me other than other humans, who are, in my opinion, not capable of 100 percent love 100 percent of the time.

I needed an unfailing power and nonhuman guidance, one that is not swayed or influenced by any one of the seven deadly sins, if you know what I'm saying. I needed something that a father—my first stepfather, my birth father, and my second stepfather—could not be. I needed something my mother could never be. I needed something my older siblings could never be. I needed nonhuman power that is greater than any power a human can possess and a love that is greater than any human can possess. Today that power is understood as anything that loves me and wants the best for me and would never hurt me, allow me to be hurt, or allow me to hurt others. Today, the Higher Power or Higher Thought Consciousness (any thought higher than my own that would better serve me and those around me) is the guiding force that I have never had before recovery but always needed.

For me self-reliance, or the belief that my higher power could fail me, could kill me. I alone needed to find my own interpretation in a God or Higher Power, which I like to leave undefined other than what I have already mentioned about God being non-human and all love, all the time, and only wanting the best for me and those around me. I often refer to my Higher Power as Higher Thoughts or a Higher Consciousness, or if you put the two together, Higher Thought Consciousness.

Nothing can keep you from your beliefs and what keeps you alive. Do not let anything come between you and your source of love or light, or a being, or just a thought that something other than human cares for you and has your best life in mind and something that will always be there for you—when you're young, when you're old, and right now.

Right after my mother left Dan, he left, or whatever happened to finally remove him from our lives, forever, I can remember the first time that I ever longed for someone. I longed for the opposite of Dan; I longed for a father. I longed for the love, the guidance, the presence of a father. My mother would tell me, "You'll have a father soon." I believed her, and soon enough, when I was six years old, another man entered our lives, a man that left a mark of both pain and joy on our lives, a man that is still living that I currently do not speak to, a man that has lost many battles and a man that has lost his oldest son (me while living), a man named Jack. (We will talk more about Jack in following chapters.)

Some of the happiest moments in my early childhood were when my mother came home with Jack, our new stepdad, who had married our mother while we were on summer vacation at our great-aunt and uncle's house in Portland, Oregon. When he opened up the trunk of a brand-new car he had bought for our mother and toys just came out one after the other, and when he bought me a Red Ryder BB gun for the Christmas of 1988 and taught me to shoot it in the backyard by aiming at Coke cans.

You may think this is harsh. How can anyone who is claiming to be in recovery not talk to one of their parents, one who helped feed, clothe, teach, and raise that person? How is this so? The answer is . . . just like every single person is allowed to have their own beliefs and dealings with, or not with, a God of their understanding, I believe in giving each other, each person, the permission to have their own beliefs about their family and what relationships are good for them and what relationships are not good for them as an individual. After all, we weren't all raised by the same parents or in the same families. Our parenting was supposed to be similar in some regard as to what our parents were supposed to have done for us, but results may vary.

I once read that the job of a parent is to make the child less and less dependent on the parent as the child ages. I would also add the job of a parent is to love their children as unconditionally as possible. Unless you believe in souls choosing to come and leave the earth, which I often lean toward, especially when a soul chooses to leave the earth (someone dies), it is the parents' fault, both mother and father, for bringing a child into the world. Should it not be the task of the parent to provide two things: education on independence and unconditional love?

I wish for so many of us that our parents were more capable, that they were not just "doing the best they could," but that they were bettering themselves if and when needed. That they were not creating chaos, inflicting violence, or raping or molesting their children. I wish bad things never happened to the innocent, that all parents regarded young life as the most sacred. I wish that in some ways, parents were not able to have children unless they could pass an exam or set of exams (mainly psychological) that stated that they could have children, or that wishful parents had to meet certain qualifications before procreating, but this would be taking away our birthright—the right to have children.

We have seen though, in recent society, child protective services stepping in, social workers making sure that parents are bettering themselves, or that in certain situations, parents are given reasons why their children are no longer theirs, and off the children go to someone else who has a better right and the heart to raise them.

If you have been hurt as a child. I wish right now, for you, that any and all of your childhood pain is somewhat lifted and that you will heal from the wounds you did not create. I will also right now apologize for any wrongdoing that ever happened to you. It deeply saddens me that so many of us were affected in such lasting and harmful ways from one or more of our parents, the ones who were, in the beginning, supposed to protect us, and the ones who were supposed to love us and save us if needed.

If you are a parent and you are doing better than your parents did, then I would like to take this time to thank you and pray for you. That you may continue to provide for your children with more unconditional love, attention, leadership, guidance, and self-respect than your parents gave you. I have no idea what it is like to be a parent—I have yet to father any children, nor do I know if I ever will—but if you are a parent, I commend you and would like to bless you. Thank you for loving your children.

THANK YOU.

There are some times in my life where I remember key moments when I did not feel loved as a child. My birth father was nowhere to be found and my abandonment issues probably start there, with him: Ken, my real father. I was six months old when he and Mother split up. Being beaten by my first stepfather is another moment when I did not feel loved. Not being a top priority in my second stepfather's mind as a small child that needed love and attention was heartbreaking even as a child, and yet another moment when I did not feel loved early on. I remember not feeling loved by my sisters because they used to hold me down and tickle me till I peed my pants, and I remember not feeling loved by my father(s). My mother loved me, and that is the only person I felt love from early on, because at that moment, those first few years of my life, I don't remember ever feeling love for myself. I do remember feeling unpleased with myself. I remember when I was in kindergarten, just five years old, that I didn't feel comfortable in my own skin, and no matter how many times I changed clothes, I still felt "not good enough."

The feeling of worthlessness or unacceptability even to ourselves, and at the core of ourselves, is possibly one of the biggest hallmarks for any addict. We as addicts recognize that nonaddicts have feelings of self-doubt or unworthiness and can relate to us a little, but to no end does the addict continue to have negative feelings about themselves resurface from time to time. It just comes with the territory.

I must tell you this now. I was sitting in a twelve-step meeting on Thanksgiving Day in downtown Denver when a man stood up for thirty-eight years of clean time, I think. He then stated the two things addicts have the most trouble with. Are you ready for this? Listen closely and read this again and again till it makes sense, and never forget it if you suffer from the disease of addiction:

> "The two things addicts have the most trouble with are change and the way things are."

READ IT AGAIN.

That sentence was one of the most clarifying things that I have ever heard in my entire life about what it is like to be an addict, to grow up as an addict, and to live as an addict, even now in recovery with over twenty-two years clean. It explains so much and so much of what I went through in the early years of my life despite never having picked up a drug yet or the shattering abuse that I had already witnessed and experienced.

> Thank you to the man who came to the meeting that day and shared this.

If you can relate to not feeling "right," no matter how "right" your life is or isn't, and you find yourself going to twelve-step meetings for years and years, while abstaining from mind- or mood-altering substances (everything that affects you from the neck up if it wasn't prescribed to you by a doctor and your sponsor, yourself, your doctor, and your higher power are all aware of the use of such substance, other than coffee or nicotine) and working the steps with a sponsor and being a part of the twelve-step fellowship and you receive way more benefits by doing so then not, then you are probably in the right spot.

I have never felt more at home with any one group of people on the planet than I did when I first started attending twelve-step meetings when I got clean at fifteen. Nowhere did people actually openly talk about hating themselves so much growing up, while using, while not using, and even now in their lives today. Addicts have a predisposition to hate themselves more than nonaddicts, for sure. I know way more nonaddicts that do not hate themselves than I do addicts that do not, even if they only occasionally feel hate toward themselves. I am telling you what I have seen, not instilling in you thoughts that you do not have. They say that the answers are already inside of us, the rest is what people tell us.

When I was seven years old I wanted to kill myself. No reason other than that is what I truly wanted to do at the time and I felt that it was somehow necessary. I was also molested by the local youth minister of the Baptist church around that same time, just after I was saved at the altar through a prayer to the son of the God of the Christian religion. I am in no way making a point against Christianity, I am just bringing up the events that took place around the very first times that I wanted to end my own life with my own hands.

I was the first one home from school during those early days of suicidal thoughts. Our mother showed us our way around a kitchen and how to cook eggs and simple things like that when we were very young. I would be the first one home, beating my older sisters and my mother and stepfather home. As clear as my day is today, I can remember opening up the drawer that held the steak knives and wanting to put one into my heart because of the almost paralyzing pain that I felt. The lump in my throat, the emptiness, worthlessness, of it all, and I remembered that prayer that I said, the one to Jesus. The one that after having said, I would be granted a spot in heaven where there wasn't the one thing I experienced in the moment that almost drove me to kill myself then: pain.

My family was in church one morning and one of the ministers said that the streets of heaven were paved with gold, that there was no sickness and no pain in heaven. I wanted my pain to end. I wanted to go to heaven, where there was no pain. If I have anything to say about the Christian religion, I will say this: life on earth as it is in heaven is not possible, apparently, according to some interpretations of the Bible, and I was way too young to understand that the goal of Christianity seems to be to be more Godlike (or Jesuslike, depending on your brand of Christianity) and have the goal of peace on earth. But not a painless earth, where there is no sickness and there is no pain.

Even as a seven-year-old boy I wanted desperately to find a solution to my problems, and hurting myself to get to a place where I would no longer hurt seemed very understandable and reasonable to me at the time, and still makes sense to me today as far as why I thought that way, thirty years ago, when I was seven.

Christianity in and of itself in no way harmed me; my interpretation of it at the time did. My lack of spiritual guidance as a troubled young boy who was beaten, saw his sisters beaten, and saw his mother get stabbed did not help the matter. Even more so, being molested by Richard McClure of Albuquerque, New Mexico, the youth minister at that very same Baptist church where I was saved in 1988 when I was seven years old, did not help. He was supposed to be the spiritual guide and wound up being one of the most harmful men to me the first decade of my life, second only to my first stepfather.

When my family was living in Albuquerque, we had year-round school. I was chosen by Richard to be one of the children (all males, he only took males) that he would take with him on road trips across the state. He was a traveling industrial salesman of some kind. We would travel across the state and he would get hotel rooms for us. I remember how fun it was driving across the state of New Mexico and even to parts of Colorado—hotels, learning how to swim, he taught me how to dive. He taught me to cup my hands in a way that helped me dive.

I was having fun and I was getting attention from a male. From an older male, I had finally gotten some attention again. My second stepfather was not known for giving me attention. I had no idea that I was being molested every night in the bed when I fell asleep. I remember Richard would cuddle with me and we would wear our underwear. I remember that I felt his genitals pushing up against my butt. I remember that one night I had a rash on my butt and he had me get on the hotel table in the hotel room and he put baby powder on my butt for me and my butt felt better. I had no idea that I was being molested by Richard. When we were driving in his truck sometimes he would put his hand on my leg, and I did not think anything of it. My parents actually asked me once if anything weird had happened while I was with Richard when I was traveling with him. They were doing their job as parents. They were making sure that their little boy was safe. I told them that he put his hand on my leg sometimes when we were driving, and they stated that that was not a big deal. I had no idea that by doing what he was doing to me in my sleep and by holding me at night in the same bed, that he was in fact molesting and violating the sexuality of a seven-year-old boy that he was supposed to not only be protecting but spiritually guiding. He was the youth minister, after all. Richard was married with two beautiful daughters. We went over to his house once to play board games. My parents knew him, everything seemed okay. The church approved of him.

My family at our best, right after she met Jack 1988/89
Left to Right: Carie, me, Jack & Susan, Hellen

CHAPTER TWO

MY SECOND DECADE (FIRST HALF): 11–15 YEARS OLD

I remember the day very clearly, when I was in Target with my mom and she told me something that altered me, utterly shook me. I was probably eleven or twelve years old. My mother told me that Richard McClure had gone to the officials in New Mexico and confessed to molesting me, her son, and other little boys. There were more than six of us, maybe close to a dozen. It was odd to hear my mother say that my name was on the list of the boys that he had molested because I never knew that I was molested until that point. I was shocked, hurt, and forever changed. After not knowing that an adult had violated me, then finding out, that had a lasting effect on me, one that would plague me for years and years to come.

I never did any research or found out what happened to Richard McClure. I'm sure after he turned himself in he went to prison—at least I hope he did, and I hope he never touched another boy or girl again.

At about the same time in my life, when I was still in my preteens, my stepfather came home unemployed. We were living in Colorado at that point. He had been fired after ten years of working for the same company. The company he worked for was called MK Ferguson. This company was one of those companies that had one of the higher-ups, like the CEO or the president, screw up and then screw everyone else under them or get greedy; the two are sometimes not separate (greed and stupidity). You know, the typical American story where one man achieves great success in a company, buys two or three houses, sends their daughters and their sons to Ivy League schools, has more than enough, and yet what they have is not enough. So, then they take from the bottom until there's nothing left to support the top and it all comes crumbling down.

"In 1988 MK suffered a loss of $3.35 per share from continuing operations and an $8.17 per-share loss from discontinued operations, in part because of a $42 million pretax loss on the disposition of its interest in the shipbuilding operation of NASSCO (sounds like a CEO or president of the company screw-up or cover-up to me)."[1]

My stepfather was fired just after that. He claims that he was asked to deposit hazardous waste or unsafe materials into the Colorado River, and because he refused this task, he was fired. I've never felt like he was an honest man, I have caught him in the middle of multiple lies many, many times, so I do not know whether this business about the Colorado River and his story are true. I may never know.

My stepdad was absolutely and terribly depressed. They had just given him a watch for ten years of service, or a medallion, I can't remember which one it was, I just remember looking at it and seeing it and knowing that he had achieved something great. He went from making fifteen dollars an hour in the late '80s as a civil engineer to making four dollars an hour polishing the floor at Sears in the mall.

At about the same time my stepfather lost his job, my mother started to openly drink and was no longer a closet alcoholic. She used to keep alcohol under the kitchen sink, with the chemicals and cleaning supplies. I remember seeing the alcohol there. And after my stepdad lost his job, my mother would openly drink in the house. At one point she would offer us a wine cooler, and I remember tasting that for the first time. I did not like alcohol at the time. Shortly after my stepfather lost his job and my mother

---

[1] Kerstan Cohen, updated by David E. Salamie, "Morrison Knudsen Corp," Encyclopedia.com, updated February 2021.

started drinking, I started smoking pot (I eventually was smoking pot with my mom).

The first time I got high was in an alley with my friends, and we formed a pop can into a pipe that we used to smoke weed out of. I would not say that my first high was a "high"—in fact, I felt worse than low. I felt insane. I panicked. My heart and mind were racing and I did not like the way that I felt. The feeling of THC inside me was not pleasant. I had a bad high, to say the least, and my two friends that got me high for the first time had to ride me home on my bicycle, on both sides of me, making sure I got home safe. I remember the feeling of the bicycle handlebars in my hands; it was not good. I remember the panic attacks (multiple), the house I got high at, and the panic attack all the way home and the panic attack when I was finally home. I did not like the feeling of being high at first, but that did not stop me from trying it again. I also remember waking up one night and in a euphoric panic attack after not even getting high and how horrible that felt. I don't remember if I woke my mom up, but it was a horrible feeling.

From then on, I was a pothead skater. I had found punk rock on the radio and punk rock shows at about the same time I started using. Skating, being a stoner, and punk rock were my life. The music that the college radio station in Grand Junction, Colorado played was the most amazing music I had ever heard, way better to my ears than the stuff from the '50s, '60s, '70s, and '80s that I had already heard. I had found music that was weird, music that was raw, and music that made me feel better than good. I've been listening to punk rock ever since (using and clean), and the funny part is, so many of my favorite punk rock bands have members that got clean before I did, in 1997, or members that have gotten clean after I did. What an amazing world we live in nowadays, where recovery is more popular than ever and it is more supported than ever.

THANK GOD.

I remember how scared I was and how exciting it was to be a part of the punk rock scene in downtown Grand Junction in those early days of using. There were people that scared me and there were people that were nice to me and music that thrilled me. There was this one band playing one time and in the chorus of their song they sang, "Jocks on Airwalks," which was a reference to jocks in high school wearing skate shoes, and it really spoke to me. I wasn't a jock; I tried to be one and was not a good one. My older sister Carie had joined the football team the same year that I did and I could accept that. She, however, played more than I did and was a better football player than I was. I think my stepdad was more proud of her than he was of me, for sure. Carie was the jock, not me. She also went to state playing on a softball team. She was an amazing athlete. I tried football one more year, in eighth grade, and got kicked off for not keeping my grades up. I wasn't even using then. There was a punk rock band that I heard sing that song "To Love Somebody," but they played it in a punk rock way. I loved punk rock. I used to get ten dollars from my mom, five dollars for the show and five dollars for a small sack of weed. I was using with my mom, anyone from the neighborhood, one of the coolest stoners in middle school, AJ, and I thought I had arrived. At that point in time, I did not want to drink or use any other drugs.

There are points in my life that I am grateful to have lived, and I am grateful that I was not exposed to certain groups of people or certain drugs. Simply grateful. I feel that if I had been exposed to other drugs enough times or other groups of people enough times, and if my mother had used any drugs other than just alcohol and weed, that I might have tried other drugs earlier on. It did not take using drugs other than alcohol or weed for me to want to die at the age of thirteen (after my first trip to rehab) when I stuck a shotgun in my mouth during a period of abstinence. It did not take using anything other than weed for my two friends and I to have the great idea to jump a railroad track in a car speeding downhill just to roll the car and catch it on fire and miraculously walk out alive and untouched other than having some sore muscles after none of us were even wearing a seat belt.

You never know with the addict. They can be exposed to certain drugs or not exposed to certain drugs and yet still find them and the reasons to use them, especially when they want them. If you're an addict or thinking that you may be an addict and you're looking for reasons to prove that you're not an addict, it's not the drugs that make you an addict. With or without the use of drugs, addicts have the disease of addiction that is unequivocally believed to be incurable, and possibly fatal if left untreated. I want to say a prayer for you that my friend said to me when I was sixteen and a prayer he said to an entire room full of people at a recovery convention:

> "If you are an addict, I will pray that you don't use, but if you use, you'd better pray that you are not an addict."

The reality of that prayer is that most addicts find themselves praying either way: for relief from their addiction or for relief in recovery from the pains of life. I would rather be in recovery praying for relief from life than be using or not in recovery and praying for relief from my using. It is sad, but it is better to be sitting in the realms of twelve-step recovery meetings thinking about using than to be using thinking about what it's like to be sitting in twelve-step recovery meetings. This, I've found, has been so true for me and countless others.

I upset my mother one day, or scared her, by starting a fire with WD-40 to cook crawdads or something. We lived on a one-acre lot that had a creek or irrigation ditch running through it, and I used to catch crawdads and cook them and boil them. My mother was also worried about me because my friends had given me a tape of Nine Inch Nails and I started to really like that band. After she heard NIN, and upsetting her with how I started a fire, she decided to take me to rehab.

It was a snowy day and the roads were moderate the day we drove up through the Rockies to Denver. I had never been to Denver, just drove through it with my family. My mother was on a mission to save her firstborn son. I was taken straight to rehab. No trip to the mall, no amusement park, nothing—straight to rehab.

We all have those moments in our lives where a shift takes place. In that rehab, the first time my addiction was treated, I remember a shift taking place. I don't remember much about the education I received on the disease of addiction or even the fact that I was an addict. I do remember this though. One day, there was this girl who was screaming and she was being held in midair by rehab staff and carried to the padded room. I remember what she said, and it horrified me. She said, "I'm going to finger myself until I bleed." I was completely shocked. I just had my thirteenth birthday in that rehab and I had no idea that someone would ever act like that. That was one of the most violent things I've ever heard outside of my home growing up. I don't remember the first time my mother said she wanted to kill herself, because she said it so often. Saying things and doing things to yourself in such a way is one of the most violent things you could ever do. I know that my mother attempted suicide when she was eighteen or nineteen, before she met my birth father. She told us the story at one point—or told me, I'm sure she told my sisters too—that when she was in college and in her college dorm or apartment, she slit her wrists in the bathtub and her roommate found her and saved her life. She said she did this out of fear of what her father would do to her for lower-than-satisfactory grades. I don't necessarily believe in shielding children from life events, but there are certain events that I wish I would have never known about. That one is among hundreds of other events that I wish I never would have known about or saw that my mother was involved in. I've had to continue to recover not only from my own addiction, but from the pain and suffering that I know my mother went through, independent suffering that I saw her go through, sometimes on a daily basis. If you have a family member that is hurt and it hurts to watch, I know how you feel. My heart goes out to you and I pray right now for anyone in your life, friends or family or even an associate, that you see suffering.

She had two other sons that she had adopted when she and my stepdad Jack were foster parents. In fact, at one time we had ninety-eight children in and out of our house in a period of three years. They were actually ranked Foster Parents of the Year in Grand Junction the first, second, or third year that they were foster parents. I cannot remember which year they received that award. They were then interviewed on a local news station as well. My parents had finally made it in some way. They were also doing Amway, which is one of the biggest pyramid schemes on the planet. They had a condo timeshare somewhere, but they had not made it completely financially; they never did. My stepdad got fired, never got a better job, and my mother never stopped using again longer than maybe six months until the day she died. The story of my parents, my stepdad Jack and my mother Susan, is a tragic story that has multiple points: a complete and total failure to get back up, failure to change, failure to hope for the future, and a heartbreaking love story of a man and a woman who, although they loved each other, they could not live with each other. I think at one point my parents just gave up on life, careers, and many other attributes of adulthood and parenthood. I knew I never wanted to be like them. I never wanted to just give up. I never wanted to be the man that didn't use but who was married to a woman who did use, a woman who cheated on him, a woman who stole from him, a woman who left him countless times and broke his heart again and again. I never wanted to be that.

It is my hope that if you were raised by parents that were anywhere close to mine or worse, that you know—you ready for this?—that you are not your parents. I repeat: you are not your parents. Just because you were raised by two people or created by two people does not mean that you are them or that you are anything like them, other than genetically and somewhat in appearance. We do not have to continue the ill legacies of our parents or our other relatives. We are all individuals. If you ever want to know what your greatest power is, you only need to look in the mirror.

Your greatest power is that you are you.

The good days that my family experienced did not last long before another tragedy happened to my family. My mother was working at a check-cashing place. She wanted to rob the check-cashing place that she worked at. One day she went in, took all the money, and hit herself in the back of the head with a hammer, and then called the police and said that she was robbed. My mother had also been writing bad checks around town. She had bought me a Super Nintendo, all the games I wanted, a shotgun, and a .30-30, two of the guns that I wanted, and then when that was all over, and maybe she thought she was going to get caught by the cops, she had to leave. She took myself and my two little brothers to Oregon, but did not tell my stepdad, and did not tell my oldest sister, Hellen, or my other older sister, Carie, who had both already moved out of the house.

I had a dove that my mother had bought me when I was about eight. It was a ring-necked dove, and I remember taking it home from the mall in a cardboard box of some kind. Four years later, after getting that dove, I had to let him go. I had to let him fly away from my hands and into the sky. His name was Grey Eagle. He was the greatest pet I ever had. He was peaceful, he was my companion, he was nice, and he used to sing to me. I would sing to him. We could not fit the cage, so he had to go. My mother took my two little brothers and I to Southern Oregon, where her father was (the man that adopted her and raised her), where she was born, and where she was raised. He was not in good health. He was also the man that while living, I think, harmed my mother growing up in ways I do not know, and will never know. He was a misogynist and not a great man. My mother went to see him while we were there. She got a hold of some inheritance of some sort, and she bought an Audi and she bought a big orange truck, a Ford I think, that had a propane tank in the bed of the truck as well as a white camper topper, for my stepdad, so he would have it when he arrived in Oregon. He was supposed to eventually come as well. It was the ultimate outdoor truck. It could run on gas or propane, and I thought that was the coolest piece of machinery that I had ever seen.

My stepdad was on his way to Oregon when his Volvo broke down in Utah, and I don't know how he got the rest of the way to Lakeview, Oregon, where we were, but he got there. Apparently, a family in Utah took care of him and wound up with the broken-down Volvo, and any and all of its contents. My stepdad must have caught a Greyhound bus the rest of the way.

All I know is I used to have friends, a pet dove, a drum set, and a life in Colorado, and it was now over. I was happy to be back in Oregon though. I loved to fly-fish and my mother would take me fishing sometimes. I found moments of happiness with my mom and the outdoors as much as I could that year in Oregon. She even bought me a pair of waterproof boots that weren't exactly waterproof, but the advertisement said they were. They were nice though, the nicest pair of boots that I had ever worn, and we were living the high life. She even bought me a fly rod one day when we were driving to Klamath Falls to get new jeans for the next school year. My sisters were gone; it was just my mother and my little brothers and I before my stepdad got there, for a little while. As soon as he got there my mother left to "go to rehab." I don't think she ever actually went to rehab, and the inheritance that she got a hold of was willed to myself, her son, and her older brother, and none of it, as far as I know, was willed to her or her sister. Her father, the man that raised her, was going to leave her and her sister nothing, as far as I know. That was messed up and completely wrong of her father. She took every bit of the cash and left nothing but the house, which was the only thing she could not take from her brother. She was generous with the money though. My mother was always generous. Her generosity was extreme, and to a fault she would give to people. Before my mother left, after having made some really nice purchases for the entire family, not just for herself, she gave me $2,000 cash in my room. I was only thirteen.

My older sister, Carie, came at one point and stayed with us for a few weeks or so when my mom was still there. My mom was messing around with some of Carie's older friends, and I didn't like that because they were not my stepdad. They were just using, loser friends of my older sister. I think that's one of the worst things a child can ever watch: their mother fool around on their father.

The worst part about being in Oregon was during a period of abstinence from all drugs. I remember quitting smoking because my little brother David had grabbed a cigarette out of my hand when we were at the park, touched the burning end to his lip, and burned his lip. I felt so bad. He was just trying to do what I was trying to do. I remember that I wanted to stop all using. I always wanted to stop using. My mother was gone, my sisters were gone, I never really got along with my stepdad for very long, and I was so miserable. I was at the lowest and most hopeless point of my life up to that point.

One day I grabbed my 20-gauge shotgun, sat down on my bed, stuck it between my legs, put some shells to the right of me on the bed, and stuck the gun barrel in my mouth. I pulled the hammer back and dry-fired it at least once to prepare. And then I heard a knock on the door, and it opened. My stepdad was home, but I did not know it. After hearing my stepdad knock on the door and seeing the look on his face (I don't know if he ever connected the dots of what I was doing), I was no longer able to kill myself. This was only one extreme day of many days and times in my life before that. I had always wanted to kill myself. I had suicidal thoughts running through my mind on and off since the age of seven, when I first thought about those steak knives. I had a knife collection, and one of the knives that I had was a Bowie knife. I wanted to put that Bowie knife into my chest by falling on it. I know what it's like to always want to die; it's just a plague, it's just a curse for some of us, and I am still trying to shake it.

Even to this day, I know that when I am in a healthy loving relationship with a woman, when my family (girl and dog up to this point) loves me and her family is better able to love me than mine, I am happier and I no longer want to die. I have something and some people to live for besides myself.

My ex's family was better at functioning than mine. When I am in a relationship like that and I am cared for and loved for by healthy people, I feel like I have "made it," and when I'm working the steps, and when I don't feel alone at home, and I don't feel like I am unsupported and unloved, I want to live. It is difficult when I am single. Very difficult. I have to work extra hard to give myself the love that I need. I am currently single now while writing this book, and it has been almost two years since I was in a functional and healthy relationship. Being single, for me, for this addict who felt like he grew up alone and who currently has no contact with any of his family, is tough. It is tough for me to find reasons to want to get out of bed when I am single.

We can only love ourselves so much, and then there lies the love of others, if and when we are allowed to receive it. Love from others takes away the times when I can't love myself and makes me feel like the times I didn't love myself never happened.

Deep and unconditional love, emotional and physical love from another in a committed relationship, changed me. It showed me how I can only love myself so much, and then there is an extension to that love of myself that only another can add, which is usually greater than my own and always greater than my own when combined with my own self-love. It is almost as if we celebrate each other in relationships, and we add our own fuel to a burning fire between ourselves and the other person, and that fire never goes out, only continues to burn, or one hopes will never go out until the relationship ends. All relationships end; that is a fact. My sponsor likes to remind me that people are in our lives for a reason, a season, or a lifetime.

CHAPTER THREE

GETTING CLEAN: 8/14/97 (MY CLEAN DATE), 15 YEARS OLD

I think a lot of my relationships with women growing up have been affected by watching what my mother did. There are some things that I could talk about that are fourth-step issues (the fourth step is where we uncover any and all of our skeletons in the closet, or issues that we feel like we should hide), and I don't know if I'm ready to talk about them in this book, but here are a few: A child is never supposed to see their parent naked and incomprehensible at any point. A child is never supposed to see a parent in their bed wondering if their parent is still alive because their parent hasn't moved all day. I used to watch my mother sometimes, when she was sleeping during the day, just to check on her in her bedroom from the doorway to make sure she had not died in her sleep. I would crack the door open and look into her bedroom just to make sure her chest was rising and falling with her breath. My mother had eventually quit working and she would just use all day, every day. Every day was the same, until one day she shot herself.

My mother and I had gotten into an argument; she was wasted and I was not. I don't remember what the argument was about, but we put our hands on each other. We put our hands on each other for the first time. She pushed, I pushed, and my mother wound up hitting the wall behind her. We both looked at each other with the most disheartened look ever. We had never touched each other in that way. We had never been violent toward each other. We were both heartbroken. I left. I had two hundred dollars in my pocket from robbing a coffee shop the night before. I went straight to the pay phone to call a cab to go use when I saw an ambulance drive by.

They found me later. My family found what house I was at and called. I don't know how, but they found the number of the friend's house I was at, across town, and they told me over the phone that my mother had shot herself in the stomach after our argument.

My mother lived that day. She lived after having the bullet removed from her abdomen and recovering in ICU. She took the bullet home with her in a prescription bottle and put it on the bookshelf in her room for all to see.

Both my parents were hoarders. It was disgusting; I couldn't wait to leave my parents' house after it got really bad in my mid to late teen years. Hoarding is an addiction all in its own. It's weird how it happens, like mice storing up as many shiny things as they can, as much insulation for winter bedding that they can, and as much food as they can. Hoarding reminds me of a purely animalistic behavior. I have had to watch myself in my adult life and be diligent about not being a hoarder (I still hoard receipts—as if I need to always have the ability to take back any or all of my purchases that I have ever made).

I wound up going to rehab two more times in 1997, when I was fifteen. I could not stand my home life and I would leave my house and commit crimes, in a small town in Kentucky, where my stepdad had taken us after my mother had left us in Oregon. He felt utterly alone and wanted to be closer to his family, so he took us to the South. I, however, felt just as alone in the South as I did out west. I felt relief when I would steal a car or break into a coffee shop. At least I was doing something, and I had a chance of leaving. I wanted to leave. I wanted something. The first car I ever stole, my friend Bryan and I were going to drive all the way to Florida but we stupidly drove past the police station on our way out of town. We were immediately followed by a squad car as soon as we passed the police station, and we were pulled over. I don't think I was actually charged, and I don't think I was actually ever taken to court on that case, but there were many more cases soon to follow, and I became a convicted felon at the age of fifteen.

I was sitting in the detective's office, nervous, but he told me to come. You see, I could not stop stealing cars. I could not stop breaking into places and I could not stop using. I had hid in the bushes earlier that week or just a few days before for at least three hours waiting for the cops to leave me alone. I was in a neighborhood where I had just stolen a car from the day before. A cop started to follow me, and I immediately drove down a neighborhood road swiftly and drove the car directly into someone's empty driveway, jumped out of the car, and ran into the field. This was the second or third car I had stolen. The next day I was looking for another car to steal and a cop pulled up behind me and a cop pulled up in front of me. They both got out and arrested me almost immediately without any questions. I literally got arrested for walking down the street. I was taken downtown and I remember this one cop saying, "That's the one, that's the one who stole the car." I told him, "No, that wasn't me." They could not hold me on anything and they let me go. So there I was, not long after, talking to an investigator in his office about confessing to all the crimes that I had recently committed in order to get out of what I was doing. I was stealing cars. I was fifteen. My mother supported me and she went up to the police station with me. Maybe my middle sister did too; I don't remember. All I know is that the investigator told me that if I confessed, he would have a petition signed to keep me possibly from going to jail. I don't know about any petition or if one was ever signed, but after leaving the police station it was a matter of days before two policemen came to my house, arrested me ,and handcuffed me in front of my little brothers and my mother.

Juvenile detention was not that bad. I got lucky. I think I was the only one in there that day when they booked me. They gave me a cell all to myself and a remote control to the TV. I don't remember much else other than what it was like to use the metal toilet with no door in front of me, to shower with no door, out in the open.

My court date was set and I was probably only in jail for about three or four days. They came and got me one day, I was wearing a striped, white-and-black shirt and pants, and they took me to the courthouse in handcuffs. My mom was there, and I had a state defender who told me not to plead guilty. I knew then and thought to myself that this guy was an idiot. I confessed to the crimes that I was locked up for. There was no way that I could plead not guilty. I went into the courtroom. The judge's name was Judge Hunt. He reviewed my case and told me that I had committed twelve felonies (all nonviolent) and that I had three to five years over my head, which would place me in juvenile detention until the age of eighteen and then in prison after that. He told me that if I were ever arrested again, between then and my eighteenth birthday that on my eighteenth birthday, I would be taken straight to prison to serve the rest of my time. Even if I were to serve the minimum of my sentence, the three years, I still would have gone to prison at eighteen. I did not want to go to prison. Because I was a first-time offender, the judge let me go on probation! I was to serve six months on probation, have a probation officer, and I was to absolutely not get into any trouble at all. That was my sentence after all I had done.

To be quite honest, I was shocked really. I could not believe that after I stole cars, broke into places, damaged property, and even stole a car from the public school motor pool and drove it through the gate, that he let me go! How could this judge be letting me go? Well, the answer is, I guess I got lucky. I got lucky again. Maybe my higher power was showing me grace? But did I stop using? No. Even at this point in my life I did not stop using—unbelievable.

I wound up violating probation three times. I had a curfew, 7 p.m. I could not stop using. I could not stop hanging out with my buddies, and one time I even left the state, which, I'm sure, was more than one violation. I was told that I had three strikes.

On that third strike, I was out getting wasted with my best using buddy and his girlfriend (the only people that were putting up with me at that point, aside from a few stragglers here and there). I really had no true friends. After I got back to the house that night, I came into the house and my stepdad said, "They came." The probation officer came to the house! It was my third strike, my third probation violation. I was to go to juvenile detention the next day and to prison on my eighteenth birthday. I had a plan.

I immediately asked my stepdad to take me to rehab. I remember looking at him intoxicated and said, "Take me to rehab, Dad." I'm sure there were tears streaming down my face; whether they were chemically induced, out of fear, or out of disappointment, I do not know. I was crying.

At about midnight we made it to rehab, the rehab that I was just in earlier that spring. Right after I went in front of Judge Hunt for my crimes, I went to rehab to make myself look good, maybe take a vacation from my home life, maybe get clean, I do not know. Getting clean might have been a priority in my life at that point, but it was not my top priority yet. I went back to that same rehab in the fall of 1997 after a summer of not being able to stay clean, so that they would not come get me and take me away. That was my plan; rehab was always a plan for something, but the result of the plan, the idea of rehab, never really stuck until this time, but not until after I was finally done using. My last use was in rehab. I had a roommate that was getting some sort of psych meds that he did not want to take. I convinced him to save them for me in the drawer of his nightstand. He did, and when I used for the last time, his pills, I have no idea what they were. I remember very clearly what I said after using them and what he said in response to me using them. I said, "I just want to be happy." He said, "You just relapsed."

I was told to mark my clean date on a calendar. I remember looking at that calendar after my last use. My clean date is 8/14/97 and has not changed since. (As I write these very words right now, I have been over twenty-two years clean.)

That third time I was in rehab, that third time between the ages of twelve and fifteen, I finally started listening. I finally started taking suggestions and the biggest suggestion that I took was going to a ninety-day program instead of just staying in a thirty-day program. I also then started reading a text from a twelve-step fellowship. I did not want to use and I did not want to go to jail, then prison.

My older half-brother came and got me, and took me to the long-term rehab they suggested that I go to. I remember smoking about twelve cigarettes in three hours on that trip. The new rehab was in the town of Bowling Green, Kentucky. The rehab facility itself was shaped like a pentagon. They had a courtyard with gardens, trees, and benches. One sunny day, a member of a twelve-step fellowship, a woman, a beautiful black woman that worked there, read one of the recovery texts I had been exposed to, to us. We all read from that book, we were all exposed to that book, but that book was finally read to me, by an addict—a book written by addicts for addicts, read to me by an addict.

We were reading from that book one day, and I remember having a "second-step" concept cross my mind, leading up to the third step (at this point if you are unfamiliar with the twelve steps, they are very easily found with an online search). I saw a strand of webbing hanging down from a tree limb connected to a leaf, hanging down from the tree like it was floating in midair, and I thought to myself, *What if this leaf was just floating in midair? What if there is a higher power?* And then I began to believe. We also worked the twelve steps in the rehab. I got all the way up into step four or so, at least, before I got out. The steps we worked were from workbooks developed by a publication company, but the idea of the steps as they were originally written was instilled in my mind. More importantly, the steps, and how my life matched up to them, was easy to see. The unmanageability, the difficulty or impossibility, really, of not being able to control my life in any way, whether I was high or not, started to sink in. The biggest trouble I had in those early days, my first ninety days clean, was the use of the word "God." How could they use this word? I was so resistant to that word. It unsettled me greatly.

I did not understand yet that the program in twelve-step recovery is a spiritual, not religious, program. I did not understand that in the third step, we, all addicts, are given the permission to find the higher power of our choice. No one's higher power has to conform to any set guidelines. There are, however, some suggestions in choosing a higher power. I chose a higher power at first that came from Native American lore. My first higher power was a bear. I had a really cool teacher, or counselor, in that rehab that gave me a book on Native American totem animals, and I picked the bear. The second step says we "came to believe in a power greater than ourselves", and the third step says we "made a decision to turn our will and our lives over" to the care of, essentially, that higher power (sub in the word "God") "as we understood him." When you really look at the phrase "as we understood him," those are just words giving you permission to pick a higher power that you understand. Again, twelve-step recovery is a spiritual, not religious, program. I finally had to understand this fact, and I finally got over my issues with the word "God." It took years. The concept was there, but the word got in the way so many times.

I had a counselor and a very nice psychiatrist. They, including the staff, all believed in me. My counselor had the craziest thing happen to him, and made me believe that if he could live through what I am about to tell you, maybe I could live through what I, up until that point, had lived through. This counselor had long curly hair. I think it was permed, and I really liked him. He was cool. He had a mustache. He was tall and he wore nice button-down shirts. He was completely and totally honest. He said one of the hardest things he ever went through was when he was in his house and someone broke into his house. He went and grabbed his shotgun, and he shot the perpetrator in the dark. When the lights were turned on, a twelve-year-old boy was lying there, shot in the head. Up until that point in my life, I had never heard a story like that. I will never forget that story. I will never forget the thought of the pain that that counselor must have gone through after realizing what he had done. It was not his fault that a child, just twelve years old, chose to break into a house, and it is not his fault that he killed the seeming threat for the safety of his family and his home. Pain is sometimes not our fault; what we do with the pain is up to us.

They told me to make meetings when I got out. Ninety meetings in ninety days is the suggested amount. They say that making a meeting a day for at least ninety days is a good idea, but so is using a parachute if you're going to jump out of a plane. I had a skateboard, and I made eighty-eight meetings in ninety days. The very first meeting I went to when I got out was a smoking meeting. Yes, back then, especially in Kentucky, we had smoking meetings. Thank God. I think the nicotine helped me stay clean in those early days, just a little bit. I am in no way condoning nicotine, just telling you my story. In fact, it was suggested that no one quit smoking in their first year clean. That would be considered a major change.

My first week of making meetings is a week that I will never forget. One day everyone came in wearing all black. An important member of the group had died. Her name was Brenda. She helped start that particular fellowship in that town and was deeply and sorely missed. I thought to myself, *Oh wow, everyone is sad and everyone is wearing black,* and I strangely felt at home. I don't mean to say that in any way that sounds like I'm downplaying the death of one of the founding members of my first twelve-step home group. I am telling you that because I was so lost, and so negative, the very color of black combined with sadness, so much sadness in one room, made me feel at home. Maybe because they were feeling.

I came from an environment where feelings were stuffed, argued upon, yelled over, over felt to the point where people got hurt, and where people constantly used over them. To be in a room full of people who shared their pain and their joy, dealt with their feelings, and shared about their feelings in a safe and healthy environment of recovery was completely foreign to me. I could also really relate to the people in the meetings. For the first time ever, really relate with people. Even though we did not use the same drugs, and I was way younger (in some cases over twenty years younger), I could relate to these people. I had found my tribe.

CHAPTER FOUR

TWELVE-STEP RECOVERY

If you are an addict, it is better to be sitting in the rooms of twelve-step recovery wondering whether you're an addict than to be out using thinking about whether you need twelve-step recovery.

We as humans have always done three things: we couple up, we tribe up, and we create civilization. There is no difference between addicts and nonaddicts in this regard. We do this because we are biologically programmed to mate, to find a mate, and we are emotionally wired to form connections with others to instill and ensure the survival of our species. Ever have your heart or chest physically hurt when you see a picture of your ex-partner, or see them in person, or just think of them with another? That pain, that physical pain, has been researched to great extent. Our bodies use pain when we separate to ensure that we as humans keep and maintain close relations. Our brain naturally produces and uses oxytocin (a bonding agent), and dopamine (a rush; addicts love this one), and other hormones and endorphins when we are physical to promote these bonds between us, and the continued use of our sexual organs to propagate the species.

We do this because the tribe and our families, or the families within the tribe, become our greatest support system. We do this because in our society, where everyone can put their resources together, usually, there is a more stable source and continuous availability of resources.

I have never found a person on the planet in my lifetime that did not take part in coupling up, finding or being a part of a tribe, or being a part of civilization. After all, those who choose not to do any of the three would not want to be found or bothered or met by another!

In twelve-step recovery, we find a tribe. We find a tribe of people who are linked. We find more than just our need for other people fulfilled, but our need for other people who suffer from the same disease fulfilled. They say that the therapeutic value of one addict helping another is without parallel. I have found this to be true. With no one else but the addict do I find complete and total empathy and understanding, complete and total acceptance, and complete and total unconditional love. Nonaddicts have totally loved me unconditionally, totally accepted me, but they have never been able to fully understand me or fully empathize with me like the addict can.

I have been in a twelve-step recovery fellowship since I was fifteen, when I got clean. I have never found it necessary to leave the twelve-step recovery process, and I believe because I did not leave, I have not used. I have found a lifetime of support within the rooms of twelve-step recovery. I know that the path of every addict is not the same and may look different. For me, I choose twelve-step recovery. I choose the connection and the unbreakable bonds that I have made. I choose "the BEST therapy in the world for a dollar in the basket," as my friend Jorge would say. I choose lifelong friendships that have lasted through ups and downs, deaths and births, marriages and divorces. I have chosen this way of life and it has not let me down. Others who have chosen the same life are my tribe, my society within a civilization.

I have seen too many addicts not only suffer, but die because they did not work the twelve steps or find another solution. Twelve-step recovery just happens to be the solution for millions of addicts in over one hundred countries all over the world. Empathy is a universal language that, when shared between two addicts, becomes a heartfelt reason of why we used and a heartfelt reason why we stay clean. I attribute all of my growth (spiritual, mental, and emotional) and my clean time to the basic foundation

I was taught to develop and the continued practice of twelve-step recovery in my life and the spiritual principles that the steps are based on.

If you have found the rooms, the rooms where the coffee pot percolates, where people are laughing, sometimes for no reason at all, the rooms where you feel completely a part of or in no way, shape, or form like you fit in, until you realize, maybe, you truly may be one of them, stay. It is only through staying through the most doubtful times in my recovery when I was young, from fifteen until I was about eighteen, that I without a doubt believed that I was an addict, that the drugs didn't matter, what I used did not matter, and that I had found, once again, my people, the addicts—except this time, we were clean. It is not "the drug" that makes the addict. When we take the drug out of us, we still have us. Addicts tribe up. We still tribe up, clean!

I remember the feeling of getting high even though I did not want to and not being able to stop. Nonaddicts simply do not have those feelings. I also personally believe that nonaddicts can use without interrupting their spiritual connection, and when addicts use, our spiritual connection is interrupted.

They say that addicts are the only people in the world that wake up and say or think to themselves, *Do I want to live a happy, healthy, and positive life, or do I want to live a negative, dark, and unhappy life?* and have a hard time making a decision between the two!

There is no mystery that the twelve steps and twelve-step recovery work. I could write a whole book just on twelve-step recovery. Maybe I will if this book does well. I will take you through the journey of what it's like to work all twelve steps in that book, but not in this one. Evidence of the positive results of twelve-step recovery can truly be seen across the globe in all races, in all countries, and in people from any and all backgrounds. I want to leave you with this: find your own reasons why or why not twelve-step recovery is good for you, and also the fact that

"OUR SOLUTIONS" is t-w-e-l-v-e letters long.

CHAPTER FIVE

TEENS: 15–18 YEARS OLD (1–3 YEARS CLEAN)

In my first year clean, I remember the first time I went to a meeting and drank too much coffee. The feeling wasn't great; it made me question my clean time, and I highly suggest watching your caffeine intake if you are an addict. That was before the days of energy drinks. Really, the only thing we had other than coffee was what we called "trucker speed," and I knew that wasn't clean. You know those little pills that they offer on the counter of truck stops? Yeah, that's trucker speed. I remember smoking cigarettes outside the front door and bumming cigarettes. I remember addicts would pick me up, give me a pack of cigarettes, and take me to the meeting. They were glad that I was clean; they didn't treat me like a teenager, they treated me like just another recovering addict. Thank God. I also remember the first day that my sponsor refused to give me a cigarette. He said, "No, you're going to get a job. I'm not bumming you any more cigarettes."

I did my best to make ninety meetings in ninety days, and it was crucial that I attempted to make a meeting a day for the first ninety days. I wound up making eighty-eight meetings in ninety days—a meeting a day for eighty-eight of those ninety days. It was stressed to me that you cannot make four meetings in two days and skip the next two days of meetings and call that four meetings in four days. It was also pointed out to me how important it was to sit in a meeting and stay in that meeting until it was over, to not go in and out of the meeting. I was told that I might hear something that could save my life. They were right. I saw other teenagers hanging out outside the meeting, and at one point there was a small group of them playing cards outside the meeting while the meeting was going on, and I remember that that was not what I was about.

Sometimes I would doodle with a sketchpad and a pen or pencil during the meeting, but I always stayed in the meetings from start to finish. Even to this day I really do not like leaving a meeting early or coming in late. I think it is very important to lead by example and show the newcomer that the meeting is a sacred place, should be respected, and should be attended from start to finish, from opening prayer to closing prayer with as little interruption as possible. I remember not wanting to get up even to go to the bathroom because I didn't want to miss something, something that could save my life. I've heard so many things in meetings that I felt did in fact save my life, and I know that there are things in meetings that might save yours. Without a doubt, I know that meeting-makers make it, and twelve-step meetings save lives.

It was expressed to me that the first year was a gift. Although that is nice to say and maybe nice to hear, I believe every day in recovery is a gift, and I will tell you that I had to work for my first year. And I will tell you that to get a year takes work—hard work. Even if you're on probation, even if you're court-ordered, getting clean time takes work. Staying clean may be the hardest thing you ever attempt; for many of us it is. I would not have made it to one year clean if I did not work the steps. I don't know if I would have made it to one year clean if I did not do service. I do not know if I would have stayed clean for one year without a sponsor. In fact, I'm definitely sure I would not have stayed clean at all (still to this day) without a sponsor.

I was also on probation, and a meeting was the only place I could be after 7 p.m. at night, and I had to get permission from my probation officer for that. I also know I would not have stayed clean if I did not call other addicts in between meetings, when I wanted to use, when I wanted to run or commit crimes, when everything inside me hurt. The first phone list they gave me, I still have today. There is one number on it that I still call. The others have relapsed, left the fellowship, or died, and the number I still call is still answered by one of the two amazing women who have always answered that line, Cindy. A funny story: Cindy's wife, Tammy, put both of their names down on the phone list right next to each other, making it look like the name "Tammie Candy", which was actually supposed to be "Tammie Cindy", which in hindsight was funny. We all three thought that was funny.

That was the first number I called. Of course I had other motivations; some of us do when we get clean. As humans we're sexual by nature, and when we get clean, well, for addicts, for some of us, that part, the sexual part, rages like it has not raged before. Not to mention I was a teenager. Tammy answered and immediately asked me if I had called anyone else on that list, and she told me that I needed to call a male. So I hung up the phone and called a male.

I will never forget the first time I reached out on the phone after the meeting and when I felt horrible before I called someone and felt better after. Sometimes the meetings would make me feel great, and then I would go home and just feel miserable again. It's crazy, but addicts are prone to making "ourselves" miserable. We just go into a state of self-misery—miserable thoughts about ourselves or others, about life. There seems to be no end to how miserable we can get, even clean if we don't watch it.

One of the most important stories that I want to tell you about in my recovery, early on, is about one night when I really needed to make a call to another addict after I was already out of the house and lurking about. I was in pain. In between my house and the pay phone, I passed at least one liquor store; there might have been two or three of them on that street. I just kept walking. I felt like I wanted to break into one of those liquor stores and use into oblivion. I also felt like I was at that first moment, the one they said I was going to have, when they say that the only thing that's going to keep you from using is your higher power. I was there. I truly believe the only thing that kept me from using that night was indeed a higher power. I made it to the pay phone. I called Paul, one of the guys from the meeting list. Paul came and picked me up in a '64 Chevrolet Impala and took me to the riverfront. We must have sat there for four or five hours even though he had to go to work the next day. I was crying and I was feeling and I was dealing with what it was like to stay clean in that first year. I was so worried about getting snot on the blue leather seats of the Impala, but he said, "It's just a car," and smiled. That love I was shown that night and the companionship I was given that night were what I needed. That night is still one of the greatest and most memorable nights in my recovery and my life.

I make sure today that if a newcomer calls and they need me to stay up with them, I do that. It is so important early on that if you feel like using to call before you use, not after. Relapses truly are often fatal, and I was afraid of dying after I got clean. I was afraid of using because I knew if I used, I upped my chances of dying. In fact, even when addicts relapse and they don't die, they still have a greater risk of dying before they relapse because of their past drug use and the toll using takes on the body. I watched my mother relapse again and again, my brother relapse again and again. The shame, the guilt, it just keeps compounding. Before I got clean, I remember the fear of using when I knew I wasn't supposed to, when I knew I could wind up in prison if I got caught, or die from what I was using or die while using. I remember what it was like to feel like using was the only answer in my life and nothing else mattered. Death was the only answer in my life that made sense. If I died while using, I did not care.

> I will pray for you now if you are currently using, or if you have relapsed, that you do not relapse again. No one deserves to die from the disease of addiction, and no one seeking recovery needs to die. No one needs to die in order for any one of us to live.
>
> If you take this concept to the edge of a cliff, no one

needs to jump off the cliff and die in order to show us that cliffs kill. No one needs to die. Please do not let the disease of addiction kill you. Make the call.

My first sponsee was actually a friend of mine before twelve-step recovery. We used to skateboard together, we used to get high together, and we used to go to punk rock shows together. I was not his best friend by any means, but I was his friend and we used together, and now we were staying clean together. His name was Chris. Chris was driving before I did because I dropped out of high school—yes, I dropped out of high school clean—and they wouldn't give me my license. It was funny, I went to the meeting that day and I said, "I just dropped out of high school" to my grand sponsor and my grand sponsor said, "Oh well." Chris was driving us to a meeting one day because he was still in school and he had his driver's license. He drove me to a meeting and in the car he asked me if I would sponsor him. I said, "Yes." Chris was my first sponsee. He did very little work (no step work) and he left the rooms and quit going to meetings altogether, and within two years, by the time he was eighteen, he was dead. Apparently, Chris was using and possibly got into an argument with his girlfriend, and then he hung himself. The church where the meeting was, where we had first reunited with each other after we both got clean, was catty-corner to the building he lived in where he hung himself in the basement.

I did not go to the funeral. I did not want to see all of the using, careless—soulless, almost—people that really only cared about one thing: anarchy. I could deal with seeing people that did not like me because I was clean. They were no longer my peers after I got clean. They quickly became the enemy, the group that I once thought that I shared unity with. It was a small town, and if you listened to punk rock, you were only one of dozens. We spent a lot of time together, the skaters and the punks. The ones that thought that they were the "real punk rockers" were the worst ones. They were the ones that took on the idea that life is a waste, let's get wasted. A popular song of the times that we liked had lyrics that said, "F*** the world, I'm hanging out with you tonight." To me, at the time, all I heard was "F*** the world." I can listen to that same song now (which, ironically, was written by an addict who is currently in recovery and has been for many years) and not be affected in a negative way.

Addicts thrive on negativity, and I had to keep as much negativity out of my life as possible. Especially early on. I learned very quickly to change my playgrounds, my playthings, and my playmates. Even a guy that I was in rehab with was not a safe friend for me when we both got out. His name was Jeremy. After he and I both got out of rehab, we decided to go to a meeting together one day, and only one of us made it to the meeting clean. His friend picked me up with him and we were headed to the meeting, but we stopped by an apartment first where people were using during the day and possibly having sex in the bedroom. All I know is, I was left in the living room to stare at a bottle of liquor on a coffee table, and I remembered hearing in the meetings, "If I don't put it in my hands, I won't use it," so I just sat there, stared at the liquid dope, did not use it, and my buddy who got f***** up at that apartment that day went to the meeting completely wasted. After the meeting, outside the meeting in the hallway, he even asked a guy to sponsor him while he was still completely wasted. I remember running up to the guy that said he would sponsor Jeremy and telling him, "That dude is wasted," and the guy just said, "Oh well."

My mother came to the meeting once, drunk, with a cup of alcohol. It was horrible, the liquid drug in her cup, in the meeting, and she was wasted! I've never seen the message take root in someone who was wasted or still using. I used to stay up all hours of the night listening to my mother, talking to her, thinking I was helping her when she was wasted and maybe I was helping her, helping her stay alive that day, but I was not truly helping her get any recovery. Recovery without clean time is impossible.

I had already been to my first convention, surprisingly, at just six months clean. And it was just for one night because my manager at the fast-food restaurant that I worked at would not give me Friday night off. I stayed up all night, went to the marathon meetings, and met a guy named Jim we called Uncle Jim (who is still clean today). Uncle Jim gave me a book and he said, "This is the best book you will ever read," and it was an empty book, just a white-on-white, blank notebook or sketchbook. He was handing them out to people out of his backpack, encouraging step-writing, I suppose.

I found journaling to be a helpful tool, but step-writing is the most effective means of writing that we have in recovery that I have seen. Whether I am writing on the concept of a tradition, from the twelve traditions, or writing on a step, "the work" we talk about in twelve-step recovery is heavily reliant upon our use of the pen and paper.

I was reading a magazine once a few years back, and I read this article about a college professor from the East Coast who did some studies on what happens to the brain when we type and what happens to the brain when we write. Apparently, when we write with a pen or pencil, we reach deeper levels in our mind than we can reach when we type. I can assure you that while writing this book right now, I am not handwriting the entire book (I'm using a speech to text tool and of course typing on the keyboard), but this is not a step, and I will also tell you that it takes me hours of meditation to remember all the things that I am including in this book, so I believe her, that professor! We get deeper when we write than when we type.

My first convention was a wondrous occasion! I met a group of young addicts from Indianapolis who let me sleep on their floor for at least an hour. That's all I really wanted to sleep that night because of how exciting it was to be there. I remember the speakers, I remember the merchandise chair for the convention having tattoos and gauges (back in 1998 before gauges were a thing). I remember talking to so many addicts, and in the morning as the sun was rising, I took a sewing kit—I asked for it, I didn't steal it—from the hotel desk and went behind the hotel to this pond and tried to catch some bluegill. As the sun rose and I was fishing, I felt blissful. All that recovery in one place in that convention center in Southern Indiana, all those people, clean!

One of the coolest takeaways from that convention was one of the trinkets or swag that I got from the convention welcoming bag. It was this little coin holder. It was my favorite color blue and it held two quarters. On one side it had the convention logo and on the other side, it said, CALL YOUR SPONSOR.

This was the coin holder that I used to hold the quarters that were used to call Paul. That night I did not use, I did not break into a liquor store, but that night used the phone instead.

I learned that service was important. I was sixteen years old with a key to two churches and I was opening meetings just after I had been six months clean. My home group had service commitments that lasted one year. That meant for fifty-two weeks you were responsible for that service commitment, and if you stayed clean in between your weekly commitments, you were automatically obligated to stay clean for that year. You would lose your service commitment if you used. They told me that if you got a service commitment instead of using, you could be of service. I heard other addicts talk about the times that they wanted to use, but they didn't use or couldn't use because they had a service commitment. I remember one day I wasn't feeling very well, possibly suicidal again, but I had a key to the meeting, and I stood there in the space between the church building and another building and I cried, wiped the tears from my eyes, unlocked the door, made the coffee, and chaired the meeting. I highly recommend that addicts get into service as soon as possible and stay in service. I then went on to become the public information chair for the area when I was eighteen. Part of that job required me to bring literature into the very high school that I used in, as well as five other high schools within the area.

My biggest challenges in those early years of staying clean were staying away from other teenagers or people that used or did not support my recovery, having to live in a house with a using addict (until I moved out at seventeen when I found a guy in the fellowship who would rent to me), and getting to meetings rain or shine until I had my driver's license, which they finally gave me after I had to have a hearing in front of a judge in order to get. Someone told me that if I went in front of the judge and asked for my license, even though I had not graduated high school yet, that they would give it to me on the basis that I needed to get to work. That wasn't true at all. They were trying to deter kids from dropping out of high school by not granting them their driver's license if they did. The judge did not give me my driver's license because I needed to get to work, the judge gave me my driver's license because I told her that I was in recovery and that I made meetings, that I needed a car and my driver's license to drive in order to continue to go to meetings. She granted me my license because I was in recovery, not because I had a job.

On my eighteenth birthday, I went to Nashville, Tennessee, two hours south of where I had gotten clean. My older brother, who was also in recovery at the time, gave me a beautiful hollow-bodied electric guitar for my eighteenth-birthday present, and I went to three different music venues and listened to music, and then I went to a twenty-four-hour coffee shop called Café Coco that is still there, in Nashville. One of the coffee shop baristas brought me a cake and a candle. I was alone, but I was not alone, I kept people all around me and I celebrated coming into my manhood clean. Just after midnight that night I went into a porno store and bought my first legal pack of cigarettes. It was a rager.

CHAPTER SIX

COLLEGE: 19–22 YEARS OLD (4–7 YEARS CLEAN)

I earned my GED as soon as the state would let me. I wasn't allowed to take the test until I was eighteen because I dropped out of high school. As soon as I passed my GED test and received my "Good Enough Diploma," I went to electronics school. It was a tech college, the same institute that the sponsor I have now went to. I applied. It was a school designed to train us to be tomorrow's workforce in the physical tech industry, meaning not computer tech, so to speak (software, hardware, coding, etc.), but actually building and working on circuit boards, lasers, electronic equipment, and computers. I learned very quickly that the math was way over my head. After six months, I had a B in Theory and a D in Math, and those were the only two subjects we were graded on. They were going to kick me out if I did not improve my math grade. One day I was in the lab working on a circuit board with my peers and I blew up not one, but two capacitors, and when the smartest kid in the class came over to help me, I also blew up a capacitor, that was it for me. When a capacitor blows up, it sounds like a .22-caliber rifle going off. Off to community college I went.

I took the entrance exams at the local community college and they said that my math scores were low and they wanted me to take math classes starting from the beginning, but that they would accept me. So I enrolled. I went to school for four years and wound up with a plain Jane bachelor's in creative writing and literature with a concentration in poetry. Lo and behold, here I am fifteen years later, after graduating with a degree in writing, finally writing a book. It takes what it takes. The rest of this book I will talk about many of my failures as well as my successes. I feel like I have just as many failures, or just "endings," to almost every one of what I would call my successes outside of my clean time. I would like to tell you that success does not make a man, calm seas never made a good sailor, and that failure is what truly makes a man or woman, but I will not. I don't believe failure has to be a part of anyone's story; whether it's in recovery or in their careers or in their relationships, it will happen anyway. Failure in life in many ways seems to be inevitable. Here's what Ralph Waldo Emerson had to say about failure and life, which I have found to be very helpful:

> Do not be too timid and squeamish about your actions. All life is an experiment. The more experiments you make the better. What if they are a little coarse, and you may get your coat soiled or torn? What if you do fail, and get fairly rolled in the dirt once or twice? Up again; you shall never be so afraid of a tumble.

Success is inevitable too. I believe what my sponsor says when he says that it takes just as much effort to believe that something will go wrong as it does to believe that something will go right. As long as you are alive and breathing and working in some way, you will achieve success in many ways. I know now that my greatest success in my entire life, personally, has been my ability to stay clean for as long as I have. I have been clean now through three different periods of my life: my teens, my twenties, and now my thirties, and it is by far my greatest achievement. I have learned that there are three times in an addict's life when it may be hard to get clean and stay clean:

> when you're young,
> when you're old,
> and right now.

Life can be hard for anyone, especially for addicts.
I also believe this:

Anyone, from anywhere, can get clean anytime.

My first semester of college was exciting! I was definitely living my dreams by going to college. In fact, the state of Kentucky paid for all four years because my income level and my stepdad's income level were so low. I only had to apply for grants twice, once for the first two years and once for the last two years. For two of those four years I had a motorcycle. I used to love to ride my bike to school. My first bike was a 1980 Suzuki 400 GN (flat black). My second bike was a 2004 Harley Davidson Sportster XL 1200 (pearl white). I played in a band called The Dishwashers, and we were a horror punk band that played all over the Southeast, and even CBGB's in New York City on a Saturday night once, thanks to my sponsor at the time (he grew up in New York and got us the show).

RIP IVAN FASKE

I had over five years clean by the time I started playing bars, and I really did not enjoy playing bars to tell you the truth. I still don't. At that show in New York City, someone had spilled an entire pitcher of beer in front of our merchandise table and there was just this pool of beer standing in front of our table on the floor. I went to the bar to ask a beautiful bartender who looked like a model if they had a mop. She had a tattoo of a single-line anchor on top of her right forearm, and I thought that was the coolest tattoo I had ever seen on a woman. She looked at me funny when I asked her if she knew where a mop was, and then just shook her head no, saying nothing. That was by far the dirtiest bar I've ever been to. I met the owner, Hilly Kristal, and asked him why CBGB's would be closing. We were there the last year they were open. He told me that they were raising his rent from $15,000 a month to $30,000 a month, and that's why CBGB's, the one and only, in NYC closed. He died two years later.

I absolutely loved playing music on campus, anywhere on campus, because alcohol and other drugs are not allowed on campus. My band won second place in the talent show my first year of college. And in my second year of college, after a solo performance, I won first place. Just me, a guitar, and a drumbeat playing over the PA.

I used to write songs about the disease of addiction in my songs. When I was in my third and fourth years of college, I used to write poetry as well. I made it my major, writing. I have found writing to be one of the greatest tools in life, and by far one of the greatest ways to relieve my mind. It's as if the mind needs thoughts to fluidly go through it, in and out, and I believe writing accomplishes this. Not to mention step work again, which is probably the single best tool in your toolbox that you could use. Addicts that formerly work the twelve steps, and then practice the twelve steps in all their affairs, are usually the ones that stay clean the longest, and hopefully die clean. I cannot say the same for the addicts that do not formally work the steps. In fact, large numbers would tell us that the opposite is true. When addicts don't work the steps, they may die.

I went to maybe one college party the whole time I was in

college because I did not want to be around drunk girls. I knew that that would be an unfair advantage because I was clean and they weren't. I found myself mainly dating a woman named Joyce, in her thirties, aside from a half dozen dates here and there with girls my age. She was older, but she was safe. I wanted love so bad. We all want love. We all want to love and be loved. I tried to make her the one and pictured myself as the man in the lives of her children that she currently had (I would be stepping in as their stepfather if we got married) and I wrote some goals down and put them to the headboard of my bed. They were probably very unrealistic goals for a nineteen/twenty-year-old, but nonetheless I was trying to be with her and I was trying to accomplish those goals in order to be with her. They were mainly financial goals. It was a big letdown when I just couldn't meet the standards that I had set for myself in that relationship. In the end, and in my last semester of college, I moved in with a girl my age named Vicky. She was the first woman that I had ever lived with. I had lived alone for over five years up until that point (from seventeen to twenty-three years old). She was an amazing woman; she supported my recovery and she was a nonaddict, like my most recent partner. I have mainly been in relationships with nonaddicts. The longest relationship I've ever had was with a nonaddict, not that there is a major difference in the success rates of addicts with nonaddicts or addicts with addicts; I just usually find myself being with nonaddict women. I will talk more about my relationships with women in the following chapters.

Just like on my eighteenth birthday, on my twenty-first birthday, I was alone but wound up in a public place with other people. I dressed up in some nice clothes and wore a very nice overcoat that I bought at a thrift store one day. I was given a pair of blue-and-white leather Florsheims by a neighbor of Tammie and Cindy's that I wore that night as well. I loved those shoes. I looked good. I felt good. My birthday is in the winter, February 25, actually, and on that day for my twenty-first birthday, the day of my birthday, I went to a play at the college, a date with myself. The play was great. I love theater and the arts and music and being around people (despite what my disease tells me). All I can tell you is, just like my eighteenth birthday, my twenty-first birthday was also a rager, at least to me.

I had to work full time while I was in college. I was a server mainly, at a steakhouse that did not sell alcohol. I did not want to work around alcohol. That way I could work in the evenings and go to college during the day. During the summers, I would work fast food during the day and work at the steakhouse at night.

I was a stick in the mud in Kentucky, for sure, in many ways. I didn't use, I used to grease my hair, my band was outlandish, and I ironed my clothes and kept my face shaved. Many women (and men) thought I was gay. It wasn't until I went to Japan and lived in and traveled in and out of Tokyo that I realized that I was a metrosexual. I remember many times while working when I was made fun of, stared at, or called a "pussy" or "faggot" under someone's breath. One time a regular at the restaurant was passing me while he was walking out of the steakhouse, and as he passed me, he whispered in my ear, "faggot." I had to stick to my spiritual principles many times to avoid conflict. Most women my age didn't understand me; it was just an awkward, and sometimes lonely, point in my life. If it weren't for the fellowship, the steps, the college (which opened my mind), my developing principles of Buddhism, and my band, I do not know how I would have made it. My college years were mild, to say the least, other than touring through the eastern half of the country in a punk rock band, but nonetheless they were difficult and I really wish I could have found a girl my age that supported my recovery, but then again, I may not have been looking.

So much of our lives, I believe (I'm not alone), is determined by our subconscious minds. In fact, some people believe that our subconscious minds are truly running the show. They say if you draw a circle and draw a dot in the middle of that circle, that everything contained on the dot is your conscious mind and everything around the dot, all that space between the dot and parameters of that circle, is your subconscious, and the conscious mind can only focus on one thing at a time. I believe step work, writing, reading, and even conversation can bring things into our conscious mind, sometimes things or thoughts we never knew existed, patterns of behavior or actions that we never knew we were capable of (like staying clean).

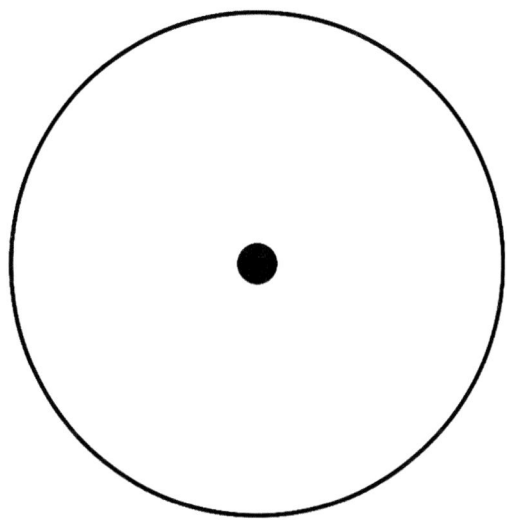

When I was in my last year of college, I inherited almost $19,000 from my great-uncle and aunt, Aunt Sylvia and Uncle Dean. I wanted to open up an all-ages coffee shop and have live music. My older half-brother had already done this for about six months and then moved on because he just moved on with things after he did them, only doing certain tasks or jobs or living in certain places for a short amount of time. He helped me open up the coffee shop though. I named it The Rock Angel Café, although we served no food. I had three or four flavors of drip-brewed coffee, no espresso, no thrills, and Jones Soda, which was a popular pop those days. I also had microwave pizza and microwave cheeseburgers. I gave kids and young adults in that town a place to hang out and listen to music that wasn't a bar. I was hated by dozens in that town because of my refusal to condone the party lifestyle, where people got hurt or were put in unsafe situations. Saw some bands would not play at my club—I would not let them play at my club either—and as a result of this conflict, their fans did not support my coffee shop. I learned a hard lesson: never let your personal feelings or beliefs get in the way of your business if you can help it. Now, that being said, I also did not want to book bands that were going to try to bring alcohol into my shop, in gas station cups like they had been doing at the hall shows around town for years. I, however, could have been nicer to the partying crowd, and I could have been more welcoming with open arms, but I still would have had to put up with their BS, I'm sure, and I tried to keep throwing people and bands out of my shop to a minimum. One of my biggest failures, epic failures, while running a coffee shop and booking bands was when I failed to write down on the physical calendar the name of a band that was to play on a certain date and instead I emailed myself the information, which is something I never did when I booked bands. The band wound up driving from St. Louis, three hours one way, to the coffee shop to locked doors. I couldn't believe it, that I had done this to a band that had traveled so far one way just to play a show. I'll never forget how horrible that felt. They called and left a message and they basically told me that the doors were locked and thanks a lot.

One day when I was in college, I was walking through the halls and I saw a flyer for a speaker that was working in Japan. I went and heard him talk about the program that he worked for, and I was in enamored. I asked questions, as well as other people, and I figured out that Japan was going to be the place for me. I was going to go there and teach English and have enough money for my bills and then save some money. He told us about how much he made while teaching in Japan, and he was making, I assure you, more than the average K–12 teacher in America at the time (in 2005) for sure. As graduation got closer, I eventually had to make a decision: drop out of college in order to further build my business, or close the business, sell off all the furniture and equipment at the coffee shop, get out of the lease, and go to Japan.

I chose Japan! My longtime friend, D, who is still my friend today, who put out a vinyl record for my band, a guy who loaned the shop money and a guy whom I believe bought my first plane ticket to Japan, a guy who now owns all record royalties to The Dishwashers (hasn't been much, sorry D), was a huge influence and support to me in my life at that time and helped me make that decision. Thank you, D.

CHAPTER SEVEN

GRADUATION & JAPAN: 23–25 YEARS OLD (8–10 YEARS CLEAN)

The morning of my graduation in the spring of '05, my girlfriend let me borrow her cap and gown that she had already purchased for her graduation, and we headed for the basketball stadium. She helped me get dressed and I went inside. I went to my spot. When I was told to, and my name was called, I walked across the commencement stage, shook the hands of the university official (might have been the president of the university, I don't know), smiled to the audience, received my rolled-up piece of paper which was to symbolize my degree (they send them out later), and that was that. I had a four-year degree. I don't remember if anyone one from my family attended, just my girlfriend's parents (who left early), and my bass player, and a few other friends and peers from class. I was happy and sad at the same time.

I got my first interview in Japan through a website that helps foreigners get jobs in Japan. After I got off the plane, I got caught for trying to smuggle in some American porn mags (I think they let me keep them, but not after embarrassing me in front of the entire airport by pulling them out and looking at them out in the open at the security checkpoint). I wasn't proud of myself in this moment, not at all. I caught a train and went into Tokyo. The lights, the sounds, the smells, all of the trees and the small houses and huge condos that dotted the landscape right outside the train windows gave me a feeling, a rush that I had never had before. I loved being in a foreign country! I felt special and really significant, like I had done something that no one I knew had done. I went to Japan!

To my astonishment, when a street vendor replied to me in English with, "I don't know you, man," after I asked him how he was doing in my best Japanese, reality set in. Although I was in Tokyo, one of the biggest multinational cities on the planet, and the most densely populated city in the world, I was still a stranger in a strange land. I bombed the interview. I was so down on myself that after five years of not smoking cigarettes, I bought a pack. A nice man from New Zealand became my friend in the hostel I was staying at. I learned that foreigners were going to have to be my friends. I had no problem with this and expected it. I was so excited, despite failing the interview, to be in a city with so many different people from so many different places. To hear them talk, and hear them talk about their home countries was amazing. After six days of being in Japan, I went straight back to America with my head held down.

My buddy Stan, my current sponsee brother, gave me a job servicing porta potties when I got back to America. I must have done that for two or three months, and then I was at his house one day and I got a call from one of the next companies in Japan that I applied to work for. I must have sent out over two hundred résumés before I got this call—in fact, I know I did. When I finally got that call, we did an interview over the phone. I did not have to fly all the way to Japan for the interview, and because the website that I was using to find jobs in Japan allowed foreigners to have a profile with their pictures up, and all their credentials, after the phone interview and a decision made on their part, I was hired. I was to leave for Japan in early August of '05. They were to reimburse me for my plane ticket after I had flown there as part of my benefits for working for them. I got a job working for the Japan International Education Center straight out of Tokyo.

When I got to the airport, my new boss, Shane, from Australia, was standing there in casual clothing (shorts and sandals), ready to take me to my own apartment. We took the bullet train two hours north to where I was to teach. He told me that he picked me over sixty-plus other applicants for the position I was given. The town I first taught in is called Utsunomiya. It is famous for Japanese dumplings known as gyoza. I knew it wasn't in Tokyo, and I had read about the problems of not being in Tokyo, not being able to make meetings, as one of the problems for people in recovery, and also being around people who did not speak English; but it was a city of a million people, so I took my chances. I never knew a company could treat you so well. I was taken to my apartment and given instructions on how to operate the apartment and its systems (AC/heat). Shane had bought me a futon, which is a Japanese word for "flat cushion that you lie on instead of a bed and bed frame," some curtains, maybe a few towels and few dishes, and then he gave me about $600 cash (¥60,000). I had truly arrived.

The next day we met at the school I was to teach at. It was a juku, one of those schools that grade-school children went to after regular school to study even more, either for college entrance exams or for their current grade level. This was very common in Japanese society. After children went to school, if they weren't on a sports team, or even if they were on a sports team, they were usually sent to study for a few more hours through the evening or the night before they went home. This was also the school where my English studio class was, which was literally in a studio office room on the sixth floor that functioned as an all-ages English classroom that I was to head up.

I enjoyed teaching. I had definitely found my calling. Teaching had its challenges, but I was ready for them. I had plenty of office hours for lesson prep, I could walk to and from work, and I was paid generously. I had health insurance, 100 percent coverage for the first time in my life as an adult.

On the top floor of the building, there was a balcony. The teacher's smoking balcony. Yes, teachers used to smoke cigarettes in 2005 on the school property. Not all of us, but I was one of the teachers that smoked. I loved my smoke breaks, looking at the city from the ninth floor, which gave me a great view. Utsunomiya is a hilly city. I have always liked hilly cities. Even the town (Athens,

Georgia) where I am writing these very words now has hills. Utsunomiya has lots of chapels, beautiful trees, and bushes all manicured carefully, the Japanese way of course. I did not have a computer or printer in my classroom, so I used my desk in the all-teacher open office. All of our desks were in an open-office floor plan butted up against each other. There were maybe ten or twelve other teachers. I was the only foreigner. I had a desktop computer, there at my desk for my use, and the first time I ever wrote my story about getting clean and staying clean was there at that desk. Three years later, in 2008, parts of my story were used in a text published on recovery from addiction. I had a lot of time to kill some days in between classes. I really only probably taught sixteen hours' worth of classes in a six-day span. Saturdays were busy, maybe the busiest days of the week, and then Monday through Friday, I had two or three lessons a day, sometimes one lesson. I think three times a week, I had three-hour classes with two little boys and two little girls, and those were my longest classes.

I was instructed to teach English only through immersion, using only English and no Japanese. I really liked the organization that I worked for. They were always taking care of me, answering the phone or promptly responding to emails. Since I was over two hours by train north of any of my coworkers, having the support that they gave me was a huge help. I really liked my students. Japanese children truly are different in ways that American children rarely are. Japanese children are typically quiet, calm, and respectful, and when they too get upset, like anybody else, it's a different kind of upset, it's a Japanese upset. It's almost like they're little samurais running around with a dignified temper. I will never forget, one time I saw two little girls bump into each other while they were running around the classroom. The one who got bumped into was the one who apologized first. I was told that when the Japanese get into a car wreck, usually the one who gets hit, if able, will get out of the car first, and be the first one to apologize, stating that they are sorry that they were in the way. A Japanese apology like that, whether they are little girls or grownups, involves the two individuals facing each other and solemnly bowing to each other. It's really miraculous to see.

My meeting attendance in Japan started out weekly. I would go to the all-Japanese-speaking twelve-step meeting once a week, when they had it. It was in the basement of a church and there was a coffee pot, literature, and key tags, just like in America, just in Japanese. They welcomed me with open arms, of course, and they would even let me share in English. I tried it, at first, to share in Japanese, but I could only say, "My name is Ryan and I am an addict and I am okay today." There was this one guy from Brazil who spoke Portuguese and he would share, too, in Portuguese. I actually understood him a little bit better than I did the other members that shared in Japanese because Spanish and Portuguese are somewhat similar and I took two years of Spanish in college. When I shared in English to a group of addicts that had no idea what I was saying, I still felt relief, and so did my Portuguese-speaking friend; I could see it on his face. I picked up my key tag for eight years clean in that meeting. After a while, the newness wore off, I couldn't understand them and they couldn't understand me, and I wound up not attending a twelve-step meeting for six months straight. That was the longest time, in all of my recovery, twenty-two years now, that I went without meetings. I don't recommend it.

I was trying to learn Japanese though and I would come home, and turn on the television, and listen to the news. That is one good way to learn another language. Just by hearing the language being spoken in the background, your subconscious and conscious mind are being exposed to it. I would also watch American movies, with Japanese audio overdubbed, when they came on TV. It really helped to recognize some of the Japanese vocabulary that I was trying to learn. In developing a habit of asking my students, or coworkers, or even people on the street a new Japanese word every day, I started to let them teach me the language. Those were my only Japanese lessons, from the people themselves. I loved learning this way, because it promoted conversations with other people.

Instead of a classroom setting where only the teacher and the student would exchange conversation, I was actually talking to real people, getting out of my comfort zone, and so many of those often-short conversations were vibrant, almost invigorating—two people that would not usually be talking to each other were talking!

Shortly after I got to Japan, my girlfriend at the time, Vicky, the first woman I had ever lived with, my last college girlfriend, sent me a "Dear John" letter. She was in Hawaii working with troubled youth, and she sent me this letter. And in this letter she stated that she had fallen in love with her boss at the place where she worked in Hawaii. I was heartbroken and disheveled, and every night for a week I'd come home and lie in my bed and cry. It was close to Halloween. One night, I decided to go out and meet people. I went to a bigger bar on one of the main streets in the city. It was packed. There was a Halloween party, a lot of foreigners having fun, and a lot of drunkenness. That night I met Miwa. She was beautiful, tall, about five foot nine, and she was wearing a long red Chinese dress. Yes, a Japanese girl dressed up like a Chinese girl for Halloween, exactly. She had a red feather in her hair. I was sitting down in a chair on the second floor of the bar, when she walked upstairs and sat down next to me. A man followed her into the room shortly after she entered, but he kept walking. I said, "Is that your boyfriend?" She shook her head no, and might have even said, "No." To my amazement, she spoke English! We had a conversation, and sadly, although she was drunk, she wound up coming home with me. I wound up carrying her across one of the streets at one point. She was laughing and having fun. I was not completely proud of myself at that moment, but to tell you the truth, Miwa and I were together for a year and a half, on and off, after that night. She was the first girl I had ever gone to a bar to meet and went home with. I do not recommend doing this if you are in recovery.

She moved in with me within a few weeks, then her dad got mad when he found out that she was living with a foreigner and made her move back home for a week or two until she and her mom were able to convince him to let her move back in with me.

    I met her family, even her father and her grandfather, and they accepted us. This was the first interracial relationship I had ever been in. Miwa's story with me ended sadly. She was saving money to come to America with me. She had a tin can with an American flag on it that she would put money in every week. She knew I wanted to go back to America and play music; I had already decided that I did not want to stay in Japan and continue to work to pay off all my debts, including my school loans, like I had originally planned, and then return to America with at least $10,000 to play music on. I feel like I have never had what it takes to do anything for very long other than just stay clean. My life is a series of short bursts of excitement, ingenuity, music, travel, and somewhat long-term relationships with women, but nothing has stuck besides my clean time and recovery. Some of the pain has stuck around too. Too much pain, I think sometimes. It's as if I have to rebirth myself, like I have to go into a cocoon and then come back out again every so often to keep my life going, to keep it interesting. Part of my life experiences have been heavily influenced by the life my parents showed me growing up: here today, gone tomorrow; and also my active mind, and the fact that I am an artist. An artist is anyone who makes art, whether it be visual, audible, or physical. I am a musician, a musical artist, a poet, and in recent years, a yogi, attempting to make my body a work of art when in a pose and out of a pose.

    My relationship with Miwa was very peaceful. It was fun and exciting. She took me up to the mountains several times to catch native Japanese trout and to go to the hot springs or just to look at the leaves that fall, that first fall in Japan. We were sexually compatible. She gave great massages. Sex and massage every day, if I wanted it—she wanted it too—and although she did not cook much, she tried anyway, and I loved to cook for her. She was a very grateful person, just a fun human being, extremely positive, and she definitely supported my recovery too. We were the same age.

For my twenty-fourth birthday we went to Red Lobster. They let me pick the lobster from the case, then brought me the lobster to check with me if that was the one, and after I approved, they cooked it for me in the kitchen. The Japanese eat a lot of different foods, a lot of weird foods or otherwise unsightly or unfit foods, foods that Americans would never eat, like fish heads, fish eyes, octopus, raw horse. They brought the lobster back to our table split in half down the middle with both halves lying on either side of a platter, and I ate everything in that lobster's shell, including the brains. The Japanese definitely taught me, and showed me that I can eat whatever I want to without any social qualms. There are really only two major issues the Japanese have with food: one, you're not supposed to walk down the street eating food, never; and two, you're never supposed to stick chopsticks straight up in rice and leave them sticking straight up, at any point, because that's what they do when they make an offering to the dead.

I struggled inside, toiled with myself about being with Miwa. I knew what touring in a rock band was like, and I knew that's what I was going to do when I left Japan. I did not want to put her through sleeping on floors and eating out of cans. I thought to myself, *She is too good for that; there's no reason to put her through that*. So, instead of giving her the option to decide for herself whether that's what she wanted to do, I broke up with her. She cried and I held her, and she left, moved out. It was sad, but it is what I felt like I had to do at the time. Often in life we have to do things that may wind up hurting other people. Breakups are known in this manner for doing just that—they hurt, usually on both ends.

In the spring of 2006, my older sister had to have knee surgery. She needed someone to help her run her business, so I took that as my way out of Japan and I left on good terms with my boss, Shane, and the Japan International Education Center. Not making meetings was also taking its toll on me. I went back to the States to take care of my sister, my nephews, and her household, not to play music like I thought I was going to when I left Japan that time. I helped her out at her business and helped take care of her small children, my nephews, and I worked for a few months until she was better, and I decided to go back to Japan.

I wound up going back to Japan shortly after she recovered, except this time I was way closer to Tokyo. I was in Chiba, which is on the other side of the bay from Tokyo. Miwa would come and visit me now and then, and I became a member of a home group for the first time in Japan. We met in a café called Mexico. Although they served no Mexican food, and what they did serve was a weird hodgepodge of Japanese and other international foods, there was a giant inflated Corona bottle above the table where we met and had our meetings. The table that we had reserved for a twelve-step recovery meeting was right below this huge, grotesque advertising prop for the liquid drug. The meetings were good and we went through a text; it was a book study meeting. One of my best friends, Jay from Canada, I think, started that meaning. He had as much time as I did. He is still clean today. Jay also convinced me to go and get a photoshoot with him to start an acting career in Japan (which I never did, even after the photoshoot, and I only went to one audition). Jay also got me into being a wedding minister on the weekends. That was fun! To tell you the truth, in all honesty, being a wedding minister was the best job I ever had. It was the most rewarding. I used to love to see happy couples, happy families, happy little ringbearer girls bringing me the ring, on what was one of the most important days of a couple's life.

I continued to focus on my goal of getting back to America to play music again. When you have the drive to play music, to perform, to tour, it just doesn't leave. If nothing else, the drive to create has always been in me, even when I wasn't touring with a band, even when I wasn't playing live. I have always written songs. I know verifiably that I've written over fifty songs, started them, maybe finished them, and I know I have recorded at least a demo version of over thirty of those songs. None that you would have heard on the radio, none that ever made it. I may die an unproduced artist, but not an unpublished author.

    I would leave work three or four nights a week and go directly to the internet café and stay up very late trying to book a new band that I came up with, Franco Funicello. I had some buddies: my bass player from The Dishwashers, Paul, and a few other guys that agreed to play with me, and a Japanese guitarist named Isamu, that agreed to come to America and do something amazing, something that had never been done before. We were to go on the biggest tour, as far as I know, that any band has ever attempted on US soil: forty-eight states in forty-eight days. I will talk more about that tour (which we completed, after playing fifty-eight shows in forty-eight states in forty-eight days) in the next chapter, and after that tour I picked up a key tag for ten years clean. I was twenty-five.

A band I played with in Japan put me on their album cover shortly after I left

*On the metro train (2005/2006)
Rockabilly in Japan never died!*

*The last year I taught in Japan in 2009
In Hokkaido (the northern island of Japan)*

CHAPTER EIGHT

48 STATES IN 48 DAYS:
26–28 YEARS OLD (10–13 YEARS CLEAN)

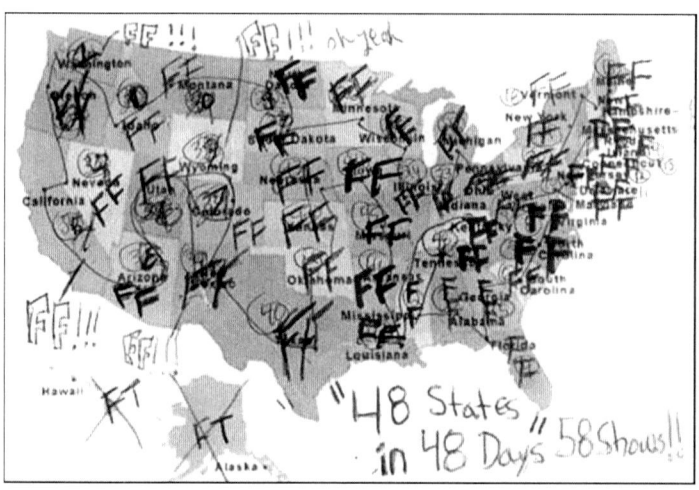

Again I found myself making plans to go back to America. I could never stay in Japan long. The isolation, the loneliness, the lack of connection with people that I had in America, just never sufficed my soul. Also, I was twenty-five; I felt I really needed to be playing music, and not settling down in a teaching career like I thought I could. In hindsight, I'm glad I chose to play music. From a financial perspective, I probably shouldn't have tried to play music for a living. Music is one of the most financially risky things you can ever do if you start with very little to no money and make it your job. Even if you spend all your money on it, and you're not a millionaire, or Miley Cyrus (whose father was a millionaire before she started, whose father also had his hand in the music business thanks to millions of women whom he swooned with his "Achy Breaky Heart" and that mullet). Most musicians do not make music for a living. I've had to accept this many times in my life.

We booked the tour. We were to play forty-eight states in forty-eight days. Although we only had just over twenty shows in twenty states booked, we were going to go on the tour no matter what. Something twelve-step recovery has burned into my mind has been, when you get something in your mind that you really want to do, something that is very possible, more than likely possible or conceivably impossible (like getting clean and staying clean), you find yourself not stopping until you've reached your goal, no matter what. Truth be told, "no matter what" is actually twelve letters long (NO MATTER WHAT—count them). In fact, there are many sayings in twelve-step recovery that are twelve letters long: "Just for Today," "Clean and Free," "New Way to Live," the list goes on. I've also found a personal favorite of mine to be "How to Be Happy." We were going on the tour no matter what.

My older sister broke her leg skiing. No kidding, my older sister had hurt her other leg and needed knee surgery once again. This time, that leg needed a lot more attention than the other one did in the previous year. She wasn't going to be able to move or get around for six weeks. I agreed to come back from Japan once again to help her, except this time I was really going to be playing the mom. I came back to America just before the biggest tour of my life and took care of my sister, my nephews, and her husband by doing the laundry, packing lunches, taking my nephews to and from school, and cleaning the house as well as taking care of her, my sister. There are times in my adult life when I got along with my sisters, when I was able to show love and care for them. This is one of those times I was able to do that for my oldest sister. When my older sister got clean, I was able to support her when the oldest sister condemned her. I miss the times when the functional relationships with my sisters existed. They do not exist today. I am the only one of the three of us that has stayed clean, and has remained in twelve-step recovery.

The band started to assemble. We all met at a friend's parents' house (D's parents' house) to practice our set in their garage. We slept in tents outside of his parents' house in the yard, showered inside, cooked inside and cooked outside, had fires at night, and woke up every day like we were going to work like every other American, except we were playing music in the garage. We had a solid thirty minutes down, but we could do an hour. We only knew two covers, a Johnny Cash song and a Billy Idol song. Those were two pretty good artists to have covers from to have up your sleeve. We could hit just about any crowd in any state with either of those cover songs. Okay, I'll tell you, because you are already thinking to yourself what songs they were. We played "Dancing with Myself" and "Folsom Prison Blues." It was the last part of May, in Kentucky. Those were some hot, sweaty practices in that garage, but we had a strong set.

Our tour manager, Evan, turned twenty-one in this time frame and we had a good time with him for his birthday—just a campfire, just a band, with our friend's dad, Billy, who came out to celebrate. Billy passed away a few years ago, and he used to always tell his friends and family that one of the greatest times in his life was when a band camped out in his yard before they went on tour.

We left Kentucky and went to Nashville, Tennessee, to record our EP for a week. Some girls that we met, probably through the studio engineer, had an empty basement and put us up in their house, in their basement, for that week while we were recording our EP. We rehearsed a few times and went into the studio. I mowed their lawn in return. This was only the second time that I had ever recorded in a studio and I was ecstatic, once again, living the dream, just like I was when I was in college, except now I was a full-time musician. After recording our EP, which contained seven songs, we played our first show of the 48 States in 48 Days tour in Knoxville, Tennessee, on June 1, 2007. There is still a YouTube video of footage from before we played that show, where we announced what we were doing to the world, that is currently still up on YouTube.

(Type https://youtu.be/BZrih7_0rDw in your search bar, or just search "franco funicello 48 states in 48 days" to view it.)

We were announcing our attempt to the world and filming the whole way. We filmed a clip from every show, from every state, to document the event, the six-week-long event of touring forty-eight states in forty-eight days. Ninety-nine percent of the clips we posted to YouTube after that tour were somehow erased from YouTube at some point shortly after the tour, possibly due to content-length requirements, YouTube's policies, I have no idea. We apparently lost our hard copy of the footage as well, and also our digital copy. To top it all off, Guinness World Records denied our attempt to claim what we had done was a world record, stating that it wasn't a world record because one man (and his guitar, no band) had toured fifty states in fifty days and therefore negated our attempt. Apparently using a plane, traveling without a band, and playing shows by himself made it an equal-to-ours endeavor. Not so, Guinness, we resent you. No, not really. They publish their own book of world records; it's not a book of public records, but a book of only the records that they want to publish. I get it. They are in the business of selling books and not in the business of making a dream of mine come true, to be in the Guinness Book of World Records.

The tour was one of the greatest experiences of my life. This wasn't my first tour, but it was definitely the biggest tour I, or any band that we had ever heard of, had ever planned. That tour really showed me the power of "we," a concept we learn in the twelve steps, a practice that humans have been well accustomed to for tens of thousands of years—we have always been stronger together than we are when we are apart. As a general rule, humans can accomplish more with each other than they can without each other. My band showed me on a daily basis what a group of people is capable of. We had to work really hard in order to make this tour possible because the tour had to pay for itself. None of us had any money, aside from a few credit cards that our tour manager and our bass player had, and very little savings. In fact, altogether, we made over $10,000 in six weeks and still came back $200 in the hole owed to our tour manager.

I have never had a greater time in my life, as far as traveling goes, than when I was on tour, especially this tour. It was a tour of the entire continental United States. I had a good group of people that not only respected my recovery, they protected my recovery as well. If we were playing a show and someone may or may not have been smoking weed, but they could smell it, they would warn me. I still don't like the smell of weed. I still can't really be around it, and I had a band that acknowledged this. It was really quite amazing. Most of the band drank, but that was it, and they supported my recovery. They didn't use any other drugs. Tours do have their difficulties as well as their joys, and there is a story about what happened the one time on this tour when a band member chose to smoke weed, and it goes like this: We had a rule for this tour the nonaddict band members (everyone but me) that no one could smoke weed or use any drug other than alcohol. At the time, in Nevada, if you got caught with a seed, just a marijuana seed, that was a five-year prison sentence. I didn't want to put our tour, and possibly put my life, in jeopardy because I was the owner of the vehicle. I did not want to put the tour or anybody on the tour in an unnecessary and difficult situation that could be avoided. We all heard stories about bands that had been pulled over by the cops, taken to jail, maybe their stuff was confiscated—it's just not a good situation that can and does happen for bands at some point if they get pulled over or they're doing something stupid. Allowing band members to smoke weed (or use any other drug), then possibly forget that they left the roach or the pipe they used in their pocket, could be disastrous. Getting caught in Nevada would have been felonious. I was firm about the other band members not using anything other than alcohol. Our Japanese guitar player, Isamu, knew this rule very well, but unfortunately, he tested it. In Florida, on around day seven, Isamu smoked weed at a house that took the band in for the night after we played to an absolutely plastered, but happy, crowd at an Irish bar. I had to do the unspeakable. I had to ask him to leave the band and leave the tour because he violated the rules of the tour and compromised the entire tour. Honestly, I made it impossible for him to stay. I told him that since he violated the number-one rule of the tour, if he wanted to stay, he was going to have to pay us, the band, to continue to play with us on tour, and also he had to agree to not use any drugs other than alcohol again. He agreed to leave instead of staying, and on day twenty-four, midway through the tour, we arrived in Evansville, Indiana, where the studio engineer, who recorded us on our EP, came up and got Isamu, as well as our Japanese merch girl, Mai. It was sad, but it had to happen.

We went from four-piece with a merch girl to three-piece no merch girl overnight. Isamu was the lead guitar player, so it wasn't a huge change. We just played the rest of the shows without a lead guitar player, and I would play the lead parts that I normally played because we both played some lead in the songs. The next show we played was a show outside of Northwest Chicago in a town called Gurnee, Illinois, where our tour manager was from. Although we had strong local support, this show did not come without its difficulties. We had a venue booked, the parking lot was full, and before the show, we discussed payment of some form with the owner, and he did not want to pay us. For most of the tour, we didn't have payment arrangements, because honestly, it's just really hard being a no-name band, just starting out, to get paid from venues. It's real simple: unless your band attracts people to the shows, and you can directly attribute the number of people who come to see the show to your band, you don't usually get paid. Unless you fill the house with fans or you're playing a bar that did well that night or the bar is generous, venues don't usually pay. I told the venue owner in Gurnee, that evening, the one that wasn't going to pay us after we filled his parking lot full of eager fans of the band, "Look, if you don't pay us, I'll take all these people that are here to see us and we'll go play in our tour manager's backyard outside on his deck." He agreed to pay us, and we played the show that night. We played the show that night as a three-piece for the first time and we did just fine. We also got a new merch girl, Hoka, who was actually seventeen at the time, but she had a fake ID that stated that she was twenty-one or twenty-two. She wound up being a huge help and just a good person to be on tour with (even if she didn't get all of our pics to us. We forgive you, Hoka).

We had some pickups (moments where our spirits were lifted) for sure along the tour, and this night was one of them. Tours can at times be completely and utterly depressing, extremely tight on funds, and very stressful, to say the least. Just after losing our merch girl and lead guitar player, our bass player's parents gave us three hundred dollars that night, I believe, and that was huge! Gas was over four dollars a gallon during this tour in 2007. We also had a van from 1984 that, although it did not need much work, we had to do one major repair in Long Island before we were done touring the East Coast. We had a leaky master cylinder in our brake system. The brakes still worked, we just dripped brake fluid from Florida to Long Island, all the way up the coast, till we had enough money to buy a new master cylinder and replace the old one. We got to the parking lot of a Pep Boys and bought the master cylinder, and then, in order to save money, I decided that we were going to do the repair ourselves, change out the old master cylinder and put in the new master cylinder. We went to one of the mechanic's bays and tried to talk to one of the mechanics about the repair just to brush up on the steps that it took to replace a master cylinder. He talked to us, but what he said was, "You're going to kill somebody!" after we told him we were going to make the repair ourselves. I think he was just trying to defend his job and promote job security for his job, maybe defend his ego, I don't know. What he said was partly true; if you do not know how to bleed the brakes on a master cylinder (which involves two people), and if you don't know basic mechanics (righty-tighty, lefty-loosey, and if you leave one of the nuts in the system loose), then I guess technically you could set up a potentially dangerous situation where the brakes wouldn't work and then the vehicle would crash and someone could possibly die.

We made the repair with great success, and stopped dripping brake fluid on the highways and byways everywhere we went. Making that repair was one of those moments in my life where I realized that people want other people to be safe; however, some people doubt the abilities of others a little too much. There were five men and one woman in that van who were all well aware of how to tighten a nut or a screw, and we were very capable of changing a master cylinder.

My other rule, rule number two, on tour was that nobody could get drunk before the set. The other band members would absolutely have a good time a few times a week for sure, but if they were going to do it, they had to wait until after the show to drink. I have never liked watching drunk band members or other artists play shows while they were drunk. That can be disastrous. Here you are in a band, a thousand miles or more from home, out there with almost no money, no food, no place to stay, and the crowds you are playing for are expecting a performance and you're depending on them. I am lucky; I got clean shortly before I started playing music. I don't know what it's like to play a set messed up, but I know what it looks like, and it's not pretty. There is plenty of footage online of bands or artists playing shows while they are high, or intoxicated, or even withdrawing, and it's just a horrible thing to see. Maybe funny to some, both nonaddicts and addicts, but not funny at all to me. There's this one artist named Elliott Smith, who is famous for killing himself by shoving a knife into his own chest, that before his death, just looked so sad when he played a show strung out or messed up. What a miserable and painful life. It's not up to us to say whether someone is having a bad time as individuals, looking in from the outside, but if it looks like a duck, walks like a duck, and talks like a duck, it's probably a duck. I have found it can be painful to watch others struggle with their addiction, even nonmusicians. I watched my mother, I watched my sisters, I watched my older brother, I watched my father, I watched my stepfather—I've watched so many people struggle with their life and cause damage in the lives of others because of chemicals. The chemicals in the brain, or throughout the body, that are released when we're touched or we touch ourselves or the wind blows just right or we exercise or we eat food or we fall in love (or we make love), those chemicals, for me, are enough. All natural highs, all happening inside the body without the use of drugs. Endorphins and hormones can also be dangerous to an addict as well. In the last chapter of this book I will talk about that in detail, about the chemicals that our bodies produce or the responses that take place in our bodies, or however you want to say it, when our endorphins and our hormones are released.

There are so many parts of this tour that I could talk about, but the most important parts, I believe, have been covered: I didn't do this tour alone, I couldn't do this tour alone, it took great effort, we were denied our world record, and we did, however, get a booking agent (that ultimately fell through).

There are a few more highlights of this tour that I will talk about. While we were headed to Oregon, we called Frank Black's house—Frank Black, a.k.a. Charles Thompson, the lead singer of The Pixies. His wife answered the phone and we invited her and her husband to come out and watch us play in their hometown of Eugene, Oregon. She said neither one of them could make it and we wound up not playing a show in Eugene but a show in Portland, right on the street, right on Pioneer Square. This was one of the funniest and most miraculous shows of all. We had originally plugged our bass amp (which had a mic input as well) and our guitar amp into a plug in a planter that was plugged up to some lights that the city kept on the tree year-round. A Portland bicycle cop came up to us and told us we couldn't play there with that power source, but we could go across the street, to the Macy's. We did just that! The department store was still open, it was in the early evening, but as soon as their security door went down, we plugged directly into the building (there was an exterior outlet), we opened up our guitar case to accept donations, and threw out a few CDs, maybe a couple spray-painted T-shirts. We used to make merch along the way, we had very little merch, and we just made it as needed as we traveled through the country, and it consisted of stencil spray-painted shirts and ripped versions of our seven-song EP in the CD sleeves they came in (we had no money for packaging). It was a Wednesday night and people just came out of the woodwork to hear us. It was strange. It was a warm summer night, but still, there were a lot of people for a Wednesday. People were dancing in the street, smiling, and having a great time with us. We eventually counted the money and we made over $250 that night, on a Wednesday night, in the street, in Portland.

We had to leave town by midnight in order to make it to Vegas the next day. This was our longest drive on the trip. People often ask me what our longest drive was on this tour or what my longest drive ever was straight through, and this was it, the drive from Portland to Vegas. Believe it or not, it's actually faster to go through Los Angeles to get to Vegas from Portland than to drive straight down through the southern border of Oregon and into Nevada. We made it, all seventeen hours! We drove straight to a bar called the Bunkhouse Saloon, and our bass player's grandparents were there ready to hear us! Aside from a few blue-jeans-wearing bartenders or wait staff (there may have only been one, now that I think about it), there really wasn't anybody else there. However, here are some pictures that have survived.

CLEAN AT 15

From Left to Right: Evan-Tour Mgr., Hoda-Merch/Photos, Me-Guitar, Bob-Drums, Paul-Bass, Paul's Grandmother (RIP), . . . and Miwa-Van (in the background, she had 7 ashtrays and no cup-holders)

The band sleeping on the floor (this is the reality of touring . . . if you're lucky)

Paul and I fronting the band (there were really two front men of Franco Funicello)

For whatever reason, I chose to wear blue jeans that night.

After the Vegas show, we had the use of a pool, a place to sleep, a place to rest, and a place to gather with family after a long drive. We then saw Paul's uncle in Palm Springs on that same tour. We saw so many family and friends on this tour. It truly was one of the best periods of my life—and I did it clean.

When I was a kid, my parents used to travel a lot, and that always meant something good was going to happen. I guess I carried that into my adult life. Traveling with a band is very reminiscent of what it was like going on a family vacation with my parents as a kid. Whatever I was traveling toward had to be better than what was behind. A new city, a new show, a new group of people, a new chance to play music—every place is always new when you're on tour. Being on tour reminds me of being a kid, the good times when I was a kid. I loved being on tour.

Shortly after we got off that tour, I celebrated ten years clean at a meeting outside of Crystal Lake, Illinois.

CHAPTER NINE

ATHENS, GA:
29–31 YEARS OLD (14–16 YEARS CLEAN)

My music career ended abruptly when our drummer left us in San Diego on one of our follow-up tours to the 48 in 48 tour and we had to use our bass player's mom's credit card to get all the way back to the Midwest (thanks, G & J). Franco Funicello broke up. Bands truly are like a marriage—they take work, they take commitment, and in fact do divorce each other, in a way, when it's over. Now, I'm still friends with 90 percent of all the people I toured with throughout my music career, but we are no longer playing music together. It's so hard for any band to stay together for very long to achieve any type of financial success great enough to sustain a comfortable life. I mean, just think about how many people want to be a musician—stay up all night, sleep all day, only work on the weekends, travel the world, and make money? A lot of people want this job. I was one of them. Most people just go on about their lives after their teens and their twenties, get a job or a degree and a job, then a partner, maybe have a few children and a mortgage. Like Jimmie Angel told me once in Japan, "Most musicians become house cats." Jimmie Angel recorded such hits like "Teenager in Love" in the '50s. He went to high school with Elvis and found a way to make music for a living, and he knows the challenges a band faces. There is a song by a recent band called The Shutups out of the Bay Area in California, and they have a song that I feel really sums up my music in my late teens and twenties. It's called "Almost Won the Lotto."

I decided to go back to school to get my master's degree about this time in my life. I was twenty-seven. I met a young woman named Jamie, who was a fan of my first band growing up. She actually messaged me while I was in Japan booking the 48 in 48 tour, and she showed up at a Dishwashers (my first band, The Dishwashers) reunion show in Springfield, Missouri, where I was sleeping on my ex-bass player Christine's couch (love you, Christine) and working on my master's. We began dating. We were nine years apart and we moved in together, and shortly after living together in her home state, we moved to Colorado. I became a pipefitter, I joined the union, and my older brother-in-law taught me basically how to plumb a house, roughly. They had a business partner (my brother-in-law and my oldest sister) who is kind of crooked, to say the least, and he wound up screwing them out of $20,000 at the supply house due to supplies for a job owed when they decided to ultimately separate as business partners. He also tried to grow weed in the pipe-cutting shop before weed was legal in Colorado. As soon as that guy started signing my checks and my brother-in-law no longer signed them, I left. I left before their business fallout hit the fan after only being a pipefitter for six months. I decided, based on talking to a band leader of a band called The Humms, Zeke, and my friend JD Wilkes, from a band called Th' Legendary Shack Shakers, that I was going to move to Athens, Georgia, where I had never been, and join The Humms. Jamie played the bass and at one time played in a Franco Funicello revival. Jamie and I loaded up our life and moved from Colorado to Georgia. Did I mention I got kicked out of grad school? I was working on houses fifty-five hours a week and I could not keep my GPA up above a 3.0 where they liked it, so I was kicked out. We drove to Athens and I found a little house, and within the first week of being there we were playing in The Humms. That's just how Athens is. If you play music and you move to Athens, you might find yourself in a band quicker than you can get your first paycheck from a new job. I just recently moved back to Athens to write this book and to possibly start playing music again, and I'm already playing in a band and I've only been here for two weeks.

That's just how Athens is! Athens truly is the "Liverpool of the South."

I only made it about six practices in The Humms and my girlfriend Jamie and I split up and they kicked me out of the band and kept her. I came home and everything was gone, except for a couch and a coffee table. She had the car. She had left me. We never really got along. We loved each other, we just didn't like each other. It was once said by a wiser person than I, "Just because you love someone doesn't mean you can live with them." I had just turned twenty-eight years old and I thought, *Wow, I have beaten all those other famous musicians who died at twenty-seven to the age of twenty-eight.* I thought to *myself, At least I can be proud of that.* But that was not enough to keep me from going down a dark road, one that I had not been down since I was thirteen years old. The suicidal ideation returned. Not only that, but I found myself in a closet with a belt around my neck the day Jamie left. I remember putting the belt around my neck and how it felt when I tightened it to where I couldn't breathe. I had twelve years clean and almost killed myself, clean. I was only in the closet for a few minutes and decided that the bar above me might not hold me or that because my feet wouldn't touch the ground it wouldn't work, I don't know, and I hated that feeling of the belt around my neck. Thank God I didn't die that day. It will soon be ten years to the day of when that happened, the day I decided not to kill myself and to push on.

When I got out of the closet, I walked to the tire shop that I worked at, told them that I wasn't going to work there anymore, and then walked straight to Nuçi's Space, which was a suicide prevention center, depression awareness, and musician's resource center that still exists today (I practiced with my current band there last night).

As soon as I walked through the doors of Nuçi's Space and told them what I was going through and that I needed to talk to someone, they paired me up with a guy named Will. I will never forget Will. He sat there with me for two hours while I was crying, while

I was telling him how bad it hurt. Why lie? I was just sharing openly, like I would be with a sponsor or even in a meeting, to an extent, and he just listened. And after those two hours were up—and he never rushed me, he never made me feel in any way that he had another appointment or somewhere to be, other than where we were in that library and in that moment, in Nuçi's Space—they hooked me up with counseling and ultimately a psychiatrist (under my sponsor's suggestion as well). Nuçi's Space saved my life. Thank you.

Nuçi's Space is actually something that I would like to see more and more of across the nation and in the world. Really! It's a place where they have rehearsal rooms for musicians and they rent out the rooms cheaply. They rent out instruments as well and there's a PA system for vocals, and it's really a gathering place for all musicians, with a very nice lounge, and there is even a stage there so they can have shows there—and there's coffee! They just recently added a recording studio, which is fairly inexpensive. Almost anyone can go in there with less than two hundred dollars and come out with a single if they are accustomed to recording. I love it. It was founded by a woman whose son went to UGA, and her son's name was Nuçi. Years ago, Nuçi was trying to make an appointment with a counselor on the campus of UGA, and they did not have an immediate opening for him. He did not make it to his scheduled appointment and he killed himself before he received help. He was twenty-two.

I was suicidal with twelve years clean; I was miserable. I had never been left like that before by a girlfriend. I was devastated. Not only did I lose my relationship, but I got kicked out of my band; they kept her and kicked me out. I loved that band, I still love that band, and I may wind up playing in that band again one day. I was definitely overdue for another trip through the twelve steps with a sponsor.

I don't know if ancient humans thought suicide was okay or if they ever thought about it as the solution to a problem for them, or if it's a modern invention, since we have been so far removed from our original intentions and ways of life. I know nonaddicts have suicidal thoughts and from time to time, they commit suicide, but I think with addicts, we almost all have an ingrained self-hate toward ourselves, and if we have made it into recovery and we are clean, we already know using drugs is not a good idea or a solution, so we either want to hurt ourselves or hurt somebody else . . . or find a solution! As addicts, when things go wrong, I think we entertain this idea in our minds and think, *Well, life's not going good with or without drugs, so I might as well just end it all, because I don't want to hurt anyone else anymore, clean or using.* Or when we lose a lover, just like a nonaddict loses a lover, that can be devastating. When we as humans lose someone we love, our hearts may hurt because our hearts were programmed to love in order to keep us together, to keep the species alive, otherwise we would have died off.

Two weeks after the breakup, I left and went to Mexico to go maybe teach English and stay with my friend Paul, from Franco Funicello. Mexico is beautiful but I could not stay, they were only going to pay me fifteen dollars a week or something to teach. There were cockroaches longer than any bug I had ever seen. The people were amazing, I never felt like my life was in danger, the weather was amazing, but I just could not stay. I could not make money there and live and work. I came back to Athens and found myself renting a room in a four-bedroom apartment with three other college students at the age of twenty-eight, and with a four-year degree I got a job bussing tables at a seafood restaurant. I worked at that seafood restaurant for one year at night and on the weekends. During the day I was a handyman for a small handyman company. Eventually I started my own handyman business in Athens, and I got so busy with the handyman business that I quit the restaurant. I wound up being a handyman for the next three years, and there's a wonderful story that took place in my life about a retired teacher named Alice and the house that eventually became mine.

When I was thirty, I was with a girl named Kay, who after

being with me for six months, knowing that my recovery boundaries required me to not live with anyone that smoked weed, got high anyway and came home. It was a Tuesday. I slept on the couch that night. She never really partied until we got a house together close to downtown Athens on Sunset. Kay came home high, we broke up, my transmission went out, and I was losing my house after she moved out and my mom died. That was one of the craziest times of my life.

The story of Alice and the house goes like this: I received a handyman call to the house I went and met Alice, the owner. She let me look around and let me give her an estimate to do the work that needed to be done. I came up with an idea that instead of working for $1,500 plus the cost of materials, that I would work for $500 a month and be able to move in there for three months with an option to lease the house for a year after three months and the work was done. She agreed. I sent her a contract for the option to lease for one year and for the deal. She signed it and sent it back to my new address at her old house. Three months after living there I proposed to buy the house from her. She said, "Let me think about it," and then it was all email from there. We began emailing each other and I offered her a price. I offered her $73,000 for a two-bedroom, one-bath house on 3.25 acres just past the mall, just on the outskirts of Athens, just on the outside of the woods, landlocking 120 acres that were behind the house. I offered her $2,000 down with "a deed for contract," which meant that a realtor didn't get any money and a bank didn't get any money either. Any of the money that they would normally get when a bank finances a house, or a real estate agent on both ends helps buy or sell the house, was kept by Alice and I. This was a good deal for her and a good deal for me. We felt mutuality over the deal. I owned that house for five wonderful years. I don't know where I was when my older sister told me, maybe at the funeral or after the funeral, how my mother died. This is how my mother died: When my EP was done, the seven-song EP, I drove up to Kentucky to see my mother and probably to Illinois that same trip to see my sponsor, and I stopped by her apartment. She had moved out of my stepdad's house and they finally separated after over twenty years of marriage. I played the EP for her. She listened, and there was something about her that day that wasn't normal. She was off. I later thought about it, and she must have had wet brain or close to it, which is a condition that alcoholics can get to at some point where, basically, the alcohol affects their brain after wearing the organ down so much with the poisons that are contained in alcohol, that brain damage occurs. She could not put an entire sentence together. She was crying faintly and looking off into the distance, and again, not saying much. She really couldn't put many words together. I left her apartment feeling off. Within two weeks, she was dead.

This is what my older sister told me about her death: You see, my mother had a pacemaker put in her in her late forties, and she was fifty-three at the time of her death. Apparently, she needed a new battery in her pacemaker. Her battery was going to go out and my mom knew it, and she just did not want to live anymore.

My mother lay there until her pacemaker stopped.

I was thirty years old.

IN LOVING MEMORY

Susan
(my mom)

CHAPTER TEN

AUSTIN, TX:
32–34 YEARS OLD (17–19 YEARS CLEAN)

At some point I had gotten tired of living in Athens, gotten tired of the handyman business, my band never made it in Athens, and I decided to move to Austin. My buddy Kevin from the program, who was a surveyor, who got clean when I had seven years clean, invited me to possibly go work with him in Texas, so I went to Texas. I was the guy that held the pole for the real surveyors, but made a ton of money to do it. They paid nine hundred dollars a week in per diem, plus about twelve or fifteen dollars an hour, and we always worked over fifty hours a week. I lived in hotels for the next two months and drove to Austin to visit, went to a meeting, enjoyed the warm weather, and fell in love with Austin, just like I did with Athens. Austin is an amazing town as well, with amazing people and great music. Obviously, they have good music because they pride themselves on being the live music capital, of not only the country, but the live music capital of the world. It's funny, when I eventually moved there, I didn't go there to really play in a band. Maybe that would happen, I thought. I really moved there, to tell you the truth, to meet women, to meet a woman like the one I was briefly just with in Athens before I left. I know, you're thinking, a guy left Athens, home of UGA, a famous college town full of Southern belles and all kinds of other women, to move to Austin? Yes. Austin is like ten times more intense than Athens—more women in their twenties and thirties, for sure, and more music!

Before I went to Austin, I was with a girl named Alex, who had two years clean when I had sixteen years clean. We met at a meeting. Remember I told you I was probably overdue for another round of steps with my sponsor? Yeah, she had more "recovery" than I did. My sponsor actually suggested that I work a step on my issues that I was having, and I did not take his suggestion. As a result of my condition ("old-timer's disease," otherwise known as ego), I only made it a couple of months with her before I broke up with her out of fear, my inadequacies, and some early childhood things that came up while watching *Into the Wild*, actually, that I had not fully processed yet. I highly recommend talking with your therapist or sponsor before you watch *Into the Wild* if you come from a violent family. The scene with the father beating the mother in front of the kids really triggered me and put me in a place that I had not been in mentally for years. Regardless of where I was mentally or where I was financially, the way I broke up with her was the wrong thing to do. The way I broke up with her was horrible. I ended up throwing the keys at her feet and basically saying, "F*** you!" and other expletives before slamming the door on the way out. She was from a well-off family, hardworking but well off, and I remember yelling, "You have five f***ing pairs of Ray-Bans!" I am not proud of that moment and I will always regret that moment. She was a good woman. The next day I went to her house with flowers. I knocked on the door. She answered, took the flowers, and held me. I didn't say anything. I left crying. I got in my van and I drove to Memphis within the next few days to get away and do some work on my buddy's condo. She did what was right for her and stayed away from an unhealthy mad man. For much of my relationships, I have failed to continue to be a stable and healthy man, but I never chose to get high over my inadequacies or failures. I've never hit a woman, and I am at least proud of these two things: one, I haven't gotten high through all the ups and downs of the relationships I've had (the breakups, the letdowns); and two, I have never hit a woman. I'm not proud of the yelling. I'm not proud of my harsh words. My biggest complaint with myself in my entire life would be how

I have treated other people badly and how I have treated myself badly.

When we realize some of the biggest mistakes we have made in our lives happened when we weren't using, this can be shattering, especially when it involves another person. Some of the most pain I have caused others in my life has been while I have been clean, particularly in my relationships. Sure, I did the most damage when I was using to personal property or physical property or to my body, but I may have caused more emotional harm clean. This may be in part because, and probably is a side effect, of coming from where I came from—wolves would have done a better job—and getting clean so young before all of my serious relationships ever took place. These facts are in no way a justification for my actions. I have truly failed myself. I have truly hated myself clean. I have failed others. It's that simple. Working the twelve steps more diligently, releasing ego, going a little bit easier ,instead of being in such a rush all the time—a rush to find love, a rush to start a band, a rush to start a business—would have ultimately led, I feel, to greater success in relationships with women and all areas of my life. Patience, it's hard for me To have patience and the willingness to believe that if I am patient, what I not only need but I truly desire will come to me has been very difficult. I do believe if we can practice patience with ourselves, we can better practice patience with others.

I condone no religions; however, I have found Buddhism and the teachings of the Dalai Lama to be the most helpful to me. I love the fact that peace and anger cannot exist in the mind at the same time. I have found this to be absolutely and unfailingly true.

My sponsor loves the Bible and the teachings within. He recently had me do an exercise with the "Love is patient" verses. My favorite part of those lines is "always perseveres." I have never been able to persevere in my love relationships with women for longer than four years (that's my record to date).

My sponsor also says (get ready for this, and read it again and again), "The only way to get good at being in a relationship is by being in one." He has been married for fifty of his sixty-eight years on this planet. He also says that it's not love that keeps his marriage together, it's his ability to deal with another person.

I wholeheartedly believe that everyone just wants to love and be loved. We all find ourselves loving ourselves in order to survive, and we find love from others in order to survive. Love for ourselves allows us to sustain our own life; even when it seems like there is no love present, there usually is. Love from others kept us alive and may keep us alive still, sometimes more than ever, from the time we entered the world. Not feeling loved is a feeling, not necessarily a fact. You have been loved by someone in your life other than yourself at some point, and that is a fact.

We couple up, tribe up, and create civilization. It is love for ourselves and love for others that drives us to do these three things.

When I got to Austin, I found Barton Springs and the creek that runs out of it. I would bathe there, swim there, brush my teeth there like a hippy, while passersby looked at me in shock sometimes. I love those waters. They are clear most of the year and you can see giant fish and all the underwater plants from anywhere close to the surface.

I was a homeowner in Athens, but I chose to live out of my van in Austin. I needed something different, and I got it!

Within two weeks I had been on several dates, and I met a very special person. A woman who has impacted me the most and loved me the most, more than any other woman, other than maybe my mother. I met Melanie. For the next four years of my life, I was happier than I've ever been in my entire life. We had a dog and we had started a business together. She was an online web developer, graphic designer, and a real renaissance woman. She could code. She could brand. She could bring a business into the light of the world in a way that no one else could. She was just an extraordinary human being. We met on Tinder, an online dating app, right when Tinder really hit in 2014. It didn't take her long before she figured out that I wasn't staying at a hotel like I told her I was, and she said, "Why don't you just move in?" We decided that by the time we met, we were old enough to know better and old enough to know whether we should move in together. We really got along, and I moved in with her and our dog (my only son), Oscar. I took her to Colorado three months after we started dating and after starting a contracting business that she helped brand and launch with me. We went on vacation to a place she had never been. Melanie, Oscar, and I, all three, had a great time, and we went to Colorado when my oldest sister was well and stable at that moment in time. She put us up in an above-garage luxury log cabin apartment. We spent seven wonderful days in Colorado, and we also saw the Grand Canyon together on that trip together. Oscar was so hot during our day at the Grand Canyon that we literally poured water on him to cool him off. I loved that woman, and in the next chapter I will talk about losing her. But not in this chapter, not yet. I will continue to talk about all the good experiences we had together, the things we did, all the places we went. At one point we toured over twenty states together as the CEO and COO of a company.

Just before the trip to Colorado, Melanie and I had our first argument. It was subtle, but intense. Like any other situation with people, when stress occurs people may react, and she reacted. She had bought a tent and some soda waters, bought us some snacks, some food, and a few camp chairs, in preparation for our trip to Colorado and was feeling a little too invested, maybe, not in the things she bought but in our relationship. I think she thought that I was just using her and that I was going to leave her after our trip. At some point she changed her tone of voice and kind of snapped at me a little bit. Not bad; she rarely snapped at all, ever. When she did, my first reaction was dysfunctional, a pattern that I had lived out time and time again. I was headed toward the door. I was going to leave. I remember something my sponsor said, something that I wish I would have done with Alex, my ex-girlfriend before Melanie, something that I wish I could have done in any of my relationships regardless of how long they lasted. I stopped. I stopped in my tracks and I stopped in my mind. I turned and I sat down at the dining room table by the door. I looked at Melanie and I said, "What's wrong?" But not in a codependent, fuel-an-argument, unproductive kind of way, but in a way that allowed her to open up to me. I was calm. This helps. Being calm and allowing someone else who's more stressed out than you that space can be taught, and it is a magnificent skill to learn. I just didn't learn it soon enough in my life and rarely saw it growing up. Like my friend Lonnie in Telluride, Colorado, says people used to tell him, "Lonnie, maybe you're the calm one on the ship." I was able to be the calm one on the ship that day. She expressed to me that her biggest fear, and what she was really thinking about while she was stressed out in that moment, was that after the trip to Colorado, I was going to leave her. She had not had great relationships in the past either. Her longest relationship was a series of ins and outs with a man that she worked with as well. The day we were leaving for Colorado was her last day working for that man. I remember in this relationship I was able to stand up for my beliefs and my standards. One of my standards was I didn't necessarily believe that if Melanie's ex had two dogs with her, that he needed to bring the dogs over so she could see them. He just wanted another way back in—that's what he really wanted. So I told Melanie there can only be one rooster in the henhouse, except I used the expletive to describe rooster. She laughed and she understood, and that really became a positive move on her part. She was able to separate from him, eventually leave him as a business partner, and started a very successful company that she still runs today that I helped her start.

We used to go to Barton Springs on the weekends and swim with Oscar, and rent stand-up paddleboards or a canoe. When Melanie's mother came to visit, we all three went out and rented a canoe. One of my favorite pictures I took with Melanie was when we were at Barton Springs and a swan floated by. An all-white swan floated right by us. It was like heaven on earth. One of my favorite movies ever is called *What Dreams May Come* with

Robin Williams. I highly recommend watching it if you have not. That swan made me think of that movie and the scenes of heaven in that movie.

We had a great life. We ate really well. We went to yoga together multiple times a week. I started recording music again. We would travel to and from my house in Athens and we always had our dog and he was always with us. The most recent saddest moments in my life have been when I think about those two, Oscar and Melanie. I miss those two.

We eventually decided to move to Georgia after I quit being a contractor and started working for Melanie. She gave me a job! She gave me a job because my back was broken when I was a kid and I was reaching a tipping point. Remember earlier on in the story, when I was beaten when I was three? Maybe that's when it was broken. I may never know. My disc between my S1 and L5 was completely flattened, and within three years after I stopped contracting, I had bone-on-bone contact. She gave me the job with her company because I could no longer physically work at the job I had. I was gaining tons and tons of weight. I would come home and eat junk food, put on some boring YouTube video about the history of Egypt, and I would fall asleep on the couch almost every night.

I sold my van to a solar company within six hours of having it listed on Craigslist, after I emptied it out at a landfill that morning. That same day we flew directly over that landfill on our way to California for my first week working with Melanie's company. We had meetings lined up. We stayed at Melanie's mom's house in San Diego. The first deal we made that week made us $5,000. After we got back to Austin, we had just as much success in Austin, and within another six months of working for the company and really learning my job, which was primarily sales, and support for her when we were on conference calls with companies, I sold $22,000 in websites and web work.

We decided to eventually move back to my house in Athens after having our house in Austin broken into. It was my fault. I didn't leave a light on like I normally did when we were traveling. We weren't in the best neighborhood in Austin, just south of First and Congress, not a bad neighborhood but not the best. Melanie liked the house better in Athens anyway, and since we could work from anywhere, we made the move back to Athens in the fall of 2015.

We decided that we wanted a product of some kind to sell online, and we got pretty good at doing Amazon affiliate stuff—making websites, adding products directly from Amazon to those websites, then driving traffic to those websites and making a little bit off of the sales. We decided we wanted our own product, and we began to brainstorm about what that product would be. Before we left Austin completely, we had met a gentleman named Josh, south of Telluride, Colorado, in a town called Rico, after we had left a business gathering that my oldest sister and brother-in-law put together. This man Josh was wearing a hat with his business logo on the hat and I could tell that he was a hunter. About that same time, the fall of 2015, I had started hunting on my land behind the house outside of Athens and filming my hunts. All that stuff is still up. It's called Traditional American Hunter on YouTube, and I had a blast doing it. Oscar would help me track the deer and Melanie helped me edit the film and build the channel and a website. That YouTube channel got more action than anything I ever did on YouTube with my music. I hunted only for food, and Melanie, Oscar, and I all ate very well from the land there in Athens, and we were moving products on the website devoted to hunting, so I had some experience with what it took to be involved in the hunting business. I talked to the man, Josh, about his logo and then I asked him how his website was doing. That was the same question that I put on a billboard north of Austin, on I-25: "How is your website performing ?" He told us the website was doing fine, and something in Melanie and I drew him to us and likewise. We all three went back to our home, and then I began to email Josh. We began to talk on the phone as well and developed a friendship. Melanie and I visited his website and it wasn't that good.

After discovering that his business platform, his logo, his website, and basically everything they were doing was not that effective, because they obviously weren't moving any product or generating much traffic, Melanie and I decided to propose to take over their company and run it and invest in it personally. It was in the archery business and we would get to travel the country and it seemed like a great opportunity to have a product of our own. This is where Melanie, Oscar, and I all three started to travel twenty states together and became the CEO and COO of a company.

I began to also professionally shoot. I was horrible. I was not that good of a competitive target archer. I primarily like traditional bows (longbows, and recurves) not compound bows with wheels and high-tension strings. On one occasion toward the end of being the CEO of that company and a target archer, I was having my bow worked on, and the gentleman that put the strings back on the bow did not put the strings back on correctly. The string popped off, hit me in the eye, and blinded me in the right eye instantly. I thought I lost all my vision in that eye. I thought I lost my eye. There was a man at that event, one of our fans of the company, that had steroids for the eye and he put them in my eye and my eye instantly felt better. The paramedics on site came over and looked at my eye and just gave me an ice pack, which leaked and then made my face burn and turn red. It didn't help. My vision came back within an hour. Thank God.

When we got back to our house in Georgia, I immediately went to an eye doctor, and from what he could tell, from the images that he took of my eye, the retina was still attached, but he recommended that I go see a retina specialist. I saw a specialist in Denver later that year and he said my retina was still attached. I still have white flashes in my eye today because of that, and the man that did not assemble my bow properly and caused the accident originally just acted like nothing happened. His whole family abandoned me. I thought they were my friends. I thought we were not only business associates, I thought we were friends. We both made a product in the same state, we both traveled the same circuits. Turns out they were horrible people, especially when money or a lawsuit was on the line. I sued them because they admitted no fault. I won the lawsuit and the lawyer handled the case out of court pro bono. It was a small lawsuit, but I won and I was able to take care of my eye because I was uninsured at the time, building up a startup, doing the deal.

I loved my job. We had some stressful moments, but we had a product, a company to really push. We were headed for great things, and possibly early retirement if we could get the product to do really well. Around the same time we took over the archery business, our dear friend in Austin, Bill, started a mortgage bank. He got the business loan, opened up shop right across the parking lot from his previous employer, another mortgage bank, and was on track to something great like we were. He, in fact, guided us in many ways with his business-savvy mind. He helped us set the price for the reintroduction of the product into the market. His startup had its bumps along the road too. We could relate to each other. We helped each other. Bill actually got clean the same year I did, except he was eighteen and I was fifteen. He was in California and I was in Kentucky. We met at a men's meeting in Austin, and I'll never forget the day I met him and he'll never forget the day he met me. I said, "What do you do for a living?" and he said, "I sell money." I thought, *What a genius.* He did in fact pull up in a Ferrari, and he always wore the nicest clothes. He said that he had never met anyone that got clean the same year he got clean that was still clean, someone who got clean before the age of twenty-one. We were both astounded with each other and we are still friends today.

Melanie always took care of me for the most part. She always took care of me physically. She was always available emotionally and was mentally stable. My inability to handle my anger, built up from childhood, often present throughout my life, and my inability to stop myself from acting out in anger, caused the greatest harm to the women I have loved and the women who loved me. In spite of working all twelve steps a few times through, in spite of years and now over two decades of work on myself and work with others, I was the one who would freak out from time to time and slam a cast-iron skillet down on the kitchen sink when life got stressful. I was the one who would yell. I have been one of the most dysfunctional people I know throughout my life, even with all the work that I have done. There is still a lot more work to do. I am still clean, and it is only by being clean and staying clean that addicts have a chance at a better way of doing things, at a better life.

Many of us have heard it said that clean time does not equal recovery. That may be true, but I will leave you with this: it's impossible to get recovery without clean time.

Melanie, Oscar and I. Steamboat Ski resort in the background '17

CHAPTER ELEVEN

LOSING EVERYTHING:
35–37 YEARS OLD (20–22 YEARS CLEAN)

In the spring of 2017, Melanie and I bought a house in North Carolina to be closer to the woods, a little bit more out of the city. We made a huge mistake and did not talk to the neighbor on the right or the neighbor on the left or any of the other neighbors that lived on our road (I would suggest never doing this). We bought the house because it was cheap enough for us to be able to afford it while we were still building a company. Businesses in the archery world do good in their third, fourth, and fifth years; we were still in our first two years. We used the proceeds from the sale of my house in Athens to put more money into the product. We were on the brink of taking our product into Walmart. I was friends with a large American manufacturer who had products in Walmart and he agreed to let us co-package with him and possibly get us into Walmart. I also was talking to a Walmart rep, and we were so close to setting up a shop in Bentonville, Arkansas, in order to better our chances at getting our product into Walmart. The product was American-made. I was told time and time again to take the product overseas and make it cheaper. I refused. I was able to keep the product made in America and also make it in America for the same price, or even for less, than what a country outside of the US could make our product for.

Our neighbor on the right was crazy and our neighbors on the left were crazy.

This is the part of my story that I don't like talking about, but this is the part that has most affected my life in my recovery—the worst part. On May 16, after my neighbor on the right, Frank, shot his gun into my backyard, after multiple times where we heard about our neighbor threatening other neighbors and Frank flipped off Melanie while she was cleaning the window and he was driving by very slowly when I was out of town, I finally decided to confront him. We had already called the cops on him multiple times for shooting his gun into the woods across the road from us. He shot his gun into land that wasn't his. He did not shoot at targets, and he was just doing it to aggravate people. However, a .22-caliber bullet can ricochet quicker than anything. I had had enough. We called the cops one more time, and the cop that came out that day said they could not do anything about it, his unruly discharge of firearms, because he produced a target in his front yard and therefore he made it seem like he was not a threat and the cops did nothing. I looked at Melanie, and I'll never forget the fateful moments that followed. Instead of getting in my car and driving by him with Melanie in the car, which I thought was a horrible idea, filming him shoot like the cops told me to, I walked over there with Melanie's cell phone on video and with Melanie standing at the top of the drive. I walked in front of Frank's house and yelled out his name and asked him if his name was Frank. He came out and said, "None of your damn business!" I then told him, "If you're shooting that way, you're going to be in trouble (pointing toward my house), and if you're shooting that way (pointing toward the neighbor's house), you're going to be in trouble." He came to the edge of his yard. I was on the road and I said, "If you come across that ditch, you're going down, you son of a b****!", trying to stop him. I had never had a grown man try to fight me after I stood my ground. He came across the ditch and came at me. In self-defense I subdued him so he couldn't get up and get his gun that was twenty-five feet away on the porch. I dragged him across the road and tied him to a tree and told Melanie to call the cops. She called the cops. The cops, the ambulance, even one of our neighbors came, a neighbor that had previously had problems with Frank. The female cop told our neighbor to go home. The male cop, there were two, a female and a male, said, "If you just hit him one time, I could see it as self-defense." I thought if he had a gun and could kill me, I should keep him from getting his gun. He had already attacked me, what else would he do? I wound up going to jail that night because the cops did not believe that I was truly defending myself because Frank had to be life-flighted to Chattanooga, Tennessee, because he had head injuries. The cop that took me in lied to me and told me that we were just going to go in and see the magistrate and I'd be let right out. I bonded out for $2,000 the next day. We had no money for that. That was the worst day of my life clean. The one time I thought my actions were justified, although violent, I was wrong. Defending my life and my family's life that day was wrong.

We were asked to talk to an investigator, told him what happened; our neighbors went to testify for us and five people from our neighborhood showed up the day of my first court date. The investigator we had talked to told us that it was going to take at least a year and a half for my case to go to trial. We immediately left our house in North Carolina and moved to Colorado. Our company we were running was facing some dodgy times as well, and Josh and his brother, the other 50 percent of the company, had actually lied about the product and its effectiveness and quality. We had a 10 percent failure rate, meaning if we took the product to Walmart and ten thousand products out of one hundred thousand products failed people, our product would be dead. We set up a meeting with one of the brothers—Josh, the man I had originally met, the inventor of the product, the man I believed in, the man I trusted—and we had a meeting in June of 2017 in Ridgway, Colorado. At the meeting, we laid out our plan to continue running the company and made it a point to go over our numbers of bringing the company sales up 1,000 percent, but we also pointed out that that was still not enough revenue. We had yet to profit. We wanted him to pay for the product's inefficiencies (his lies), and we told him it was going to cost about $90,000 to fix the product issues before it went to the masses and went into big box stores and he refused. We left. We left the company. We lost.

In hindsight, I will tell you this: sometimes you can wind up shaking hands with the wrong man. I shook hands with the wrong man. I could be mad at God all day long. I could ask God, "Why?" all day long, but asking God, "Why?" is like throwing a rock up in the air, watching it fall, and asking God, "Why did the rock fall?" As much as gravity exists, so do dishonest people. Sometimes we don't know who is dishonest or who his honest, even in the middle of a partnership that seems to be going well. Dishonesty can come around and bite you in the ass. Within less than a year and a half of leaving that company, both brothers closed the doors, stopped manufacturing, and the product is now truly dead.

Melanie and I did what we normally do, we worked hard and we went back to work on the company that we originally started together. We sold and built a website for a prominent rehab in Steamboat Springs. I celebrated twenty years clean in Steamboat Springs, Colorado, in the fall of 2017. We also sold and built a website for a prominent member in the worldwide recovery community and treatment community. He was actually the spokesperson for a lot of companies when it came to the opiate crisis. His name is Austin Eubanks. He was a Columbine shooting survivor and he was in recovery when I met him. Or so I thought. The day I met him, we were consulting him about his personal website. I asked how long he had been in recovery; he said, "Seven years." I asked him how many meetings he went to and he said he didn't really go to meetings anymore, that he just met up with his friends from rehab a few times a year. I thought to myself, *Well, that's not recovery*. But who am I to judge? Another man's recovery is another man's recovery, and my recovery is up to me, not up to him, and vice versa.

Austin died within two years of meeting him. He died of an overdose. He went back to using, and in fact, he did a TED Talk just before he died on the opiate crisis in America. I was deeply saddened after I watched that TED Talk because I watched it postmortem. He was a good man, but plenty of good people, men and women, die from the disease of addiction every single day all over the world. The foundation for all of humanity is goodness. I believe that we are all good in the core of our beings. After all, like Neale Donald Walsch says, something to the effect of we are all teacups on the beach filled with salt water and God is the ocean and I believe God is love (I'm paraphrasing), but in spite of being a good person, the disease does not care how good we are. The disease is also always stronger than us by ourselves alone and wants to get us alone before it tries to kill us. I truly believe that Austin was alone, that he had maybe reached a level of fame, prestige, or popularity that kept him from reaching out. Maybe his ego took its hold? I will never know. The day I met him, I compared myself to him. I looked at his girlfriend, she was younger than mine. I looked at his tattoos, they were nicer than mine. I looked at her brand-new condo, it was nicer than anything I had ever lived in; and I looked at his job, he was the CEO of a prominent treatment center in ski-town USA. I thought, *What a life. He is so lucky.* We are all lucky if we survive dying from the disease of addiction, but it is not luck that will keep us here, it is hard work. Despite my many failures, despite hate for myself (which I experience from time to time even today), I have had to continue to work on my positive attributes, the person that I will be tomorrow that I may not be today. In fact, if you kill the person you are now, you are also killing the person you could be tomorrow. I try not to compare myself to others, but it happens. I have found it futile at best. Like my buddy Brendan in Denver says, "The only person I need to compare myself to is the fool I was yesterday."

When a drug addict dies of an overdose or from their own hands, it is a senseless death. An unnecessary death. Again, no addict needs to die so another addict can live. The disease kills some of us anyway. Not everyone is willing to do the work, and that's the cold hard truth. Honest willingness to continue to learn and to not be alone, to shatter our ego, is the best place to be. My sponsor always says, "Always remain teachable." Austin was found dead and alone. He wasn't the first, and I'm sure he won't be the last. Don't let your body be the next one found. Do what it takes to not be alone. Do what it takes to stay clean in order to live.

I will pray that you never use again.

In fact, addicts that live the twelve-step program never relapse. We have never seen a person who lives a twelve-step program relapse, because if you're living the program, you won't use. Living the program simply means you don't use along with everything else that is suggested, but you have to not use in order to do everything else that the program entails. It is impossible to use and recover at the same time.

I started sponsoring people immediately before and after Melanie left. In that first year of being single and while going through all the things I was about to go through—back surgery, finding a new place to live, finding another career—I was able to help three guys in Denver work the steps and get through their first year clean. I still have one of those sponsees today, and as far as I know, the other two are still clean. It is only because I was helped that I am able to help others. In order to keep our own recovery going, it is absolutely imperative that we help others to keep their recovery as well.

I am obviously not perfect. No perfect addict exists. No perfect human exists. I began to lose everything, my business, my freedom for a night, and then I lost Melanie, my dog Oscar, my Mini Cooper, and my house. Then my father died. I still didn't use. I still had a chance at life. I still chose to live the program no matter what I had done, no matter what was done to me. I wasn't a failure at living the program. The only true failure we can ever have in recovery is a relapse. Everything else is, yes, trial and error, but not a true failure. I may not be the best person sometimes, in the times when it matters most—the best businessman, the best boyfriend—but I refuse to use. I refuse to get high and I refuse to kill myself. The program involves me not using and not killing myself. It also involves me helping others, being there for others, no matter what I am going through.

A friend of mine, Janice in Denver, says, "It's not what you're dealt, it's what you do."

The day Melanie left, I drove to Illinois to say goodbye to a dying man who was my father, a dying man I never really knew. I came back, and I had three months left in the place that I was living in and then I had to go have back surgery in order to fix the part of my back that my first stepfather had broken. Melanie was such an amazing person. She helped me get insurance for the back surgery before we broke up. It was a $95,000 back surgery. I had some friends who have been like family to me from the Catholic church in Telluride, Colorado that put me up and gave me a place to go in Grand Junction, Colorado after the back surgery, when I needed to rest before I was able to drive. They also provided me a place in Telluride for five months after my back surgery to give me a place to heal. Melanie continued to deposit money into my bank account all the way up until the week I was in the hospital for my back surgery.

My sponsor had experienced back surgery, and he was certain that I was going to have to withdraw from opiates, that I was going to have to take something for the pain. I had literature from several 12-step fellowships about what it's like to have to inform your doctor, your higher power, yourself and your sponsor about a decision to use pain medication if and when needed in order to allow the body to heal, not to get high. I am lucky. I did not have to take any opiates after surgery. Although the hospital staff offered me opiates on three different occasions in just 24 hours, I refused to take them. I survived back surgery without having to use pain medication by using the prescribed amount of Tylenol, two different non-narcotic muscle relaxers, the ice packs and allowing myself to feel the most physical pain that I have ever felt, and I ate the sherbet! I would just sit there and cry and eat the sherbet. I left the hospital without a script. They would have given me one, just in case I needed it, though I didn't need it.

THANK GOD.

As soon as I got back to Denver, I continued to dig into the fellowship. I wound up having to drive Uber for nine months. I went from being a CEO of a company to an Uber driver. After Melanie and I left North Carolina, we left our business partners, we broke up, and I had back surgery, Melanie and I lost a total of $379,000 in property, compensation, and assets within one year. It was stifling and paralyzing to have gone through all of that, but I did not use.

I thought, I have gone through so many struggles, from the age of 3, so many struggles and now these struggles?

One thing I've learned for sure in life: it's not what you do, it's who you are when you're doing it. My friend Bill from Austin would call me when I was completely depressed. Not only was I now an Uber driver, single, living in a not-so-nice studio apartment alone, single for the first time in four years, but I was also completely and totally torn down. I was torn down to the point of nothingness. Suicidal ideation obviously returned. I don't know what it is with this addict, but I have had a love affair with my own death for the majority of my life. It's not me that I want to kill, it's the pain. The pain of being alone. The pain of being hurt. The pain of not being able to change where I came from, or sometimes, I feel, where I'm going. If you're an addict and you're reading this now, you know the pain, the endless pain that's always there, but we don't always feel it, but we can when we choose to or when different life experiences bring it up. We don't need to always be able to feel and re-feel the pains of life; we lived it and we will continue to live through any pain we may encounter. That is the hope anyway. Life truly is both equal parts pain and joy. I truly believe this, and I refused to believe this for so much of my recovery. From time to time I still feel the pain. I'm feeling the pain right now as I cry and I tell you all of this.

Bill would call me and check on me, sometimes daily, while I was hurting the most. I still talked to my sponsor. I still went to local meetings. I still sponsored people. I still showed up. I was still working steps on paper. I never gave up. Even when I got punched in the face while driving for Uber, even when someone threw up in my car, even when I put up with drunk couples fighting in the backseat, I persevered and kept that job until the state of North Carolina took that job from me.

I lost my self-defense case two and a half years after I was charged with a crime that I could not get dropped because I could not afford a good enough attorney and because of the cop's decision to push the charge officially given to me by the magistrate, and then making the case *Ryan v. North Carolina*. My attorney was going to cost $15,000 at a minimum. And that would not have even gotten me the best attorney. Melanie had to get an attorney, too, because they charged her with obstruction of justice after she deleted the part of the cell phone video before I threw it down where I said, "If you come across that ditch, you're going down, you son of a b****." We both had to get attorneys. I had one from the state and she had one that cost $5,000 that her mom helped her get. Melanie never had to come back to North Carolina for any of the court dates after we broke up. I spent thousands of dollars traveling to and from North Carolina anyway, only to eventually lose. When I lost my self-defense case, they locked me up for fourteen days, the minimum sentence for assault with injury, and they gave me a misdemeanor. When you have a misdemeanor, a violent misdemeanor, pop up on your record, Uber fires you instantly. They deactivate you. When I got out of jail after being locked up with twenty-two years clean, never in a million years thinking that I would ever be locked up again after getting clean and then getting locked up not once, but twice, I was shattered. I drove back to Colorado just broken, but happy that I was not ultimately convicted of a felony, which was the original charge.

I got back to Denver and I woke up jobless, with an eviction notice on my door, and a bill for the state of North Carolina for $3,200. Because I lost my case, I had to pay for my attorney, court fees, and my jail time.

I started contracting again in order to pay that fine, keep my apartment, keep my vehicle, and keep my life together. Bill, from

Austin, coached me again in business, like he always had, since the day I met him. And with his guidance, I was able to come up with $6,000 in six weeks and stay afloat. I blew up the contracting business, launched a Facebook page, used online apps to get jobs, and kept my paintbrush on the wall. I made about $8,000 in the next two months after the first month of contracting again. My body really couldn't handle it, even over a year and a half out from the surgery, so after I hired over a half dozen other men and women to help me finish my contracts, I stopped and I decided to go back to Athens and to write this book.

Before I came back to Athens, I spent this last Christmas with Paul, from Franco Funicello and his family northwest of Chicago. I spent four days with a large family and their children. I ate perogies for the first time, I really had a good time. I held a baby, played their family Christmas games and had several nights of laughs and great conversations with a functional and healthy group of people, a well and healthy family, a small tribe.

As soon as I got on the plane, I felt the absolute loneliness that I had felt for the last twenty-two months of being single and no longer having any family in my life, no longer having someone to come home to. I missed Oscar, I missed Melanie. I saw a woman crying in the Chicago airport just before my flight took off. I wondered if that was why she was crying too, because she was also alone.

CHAPTER TWELVE

IN CLOSING

In my life, I have lost so much. Getting clean young and staying clean has not saved me from going through the ups and downs of life. My clean time is the only treasure that truly matters here on earth, in this life and I have yet to lose that. I am not expecting another life after this life or a better one in heaven. For me this is it. What I do with my life has, and always will, depend on my recovery and staying clean, no matter what. I truly believe that anyone, from anywhere, can get clean anytime, and staying clean should always be an addict's first priority. Without clean time, we have nothing, and our chances of any success in our lives shrink drastically if we use again or in some cases, our life ends.

I would like to thank you for allowing me to share my recovery with you, my failures and my successes. I would like to thank you for your love and compassion. Not only your love and compassion for me, because you bought this book, but for your love and compassion for all addicts and all people everywhere. Like minds seek like minds. We are all in this life together and we gravitate toward our tribe, our people, other addicts and nonaddict that truly are amazing people, even if they don't share our disease.

I would like to now focus on some things that I have had to have patience with and compassion with, compassion and patience for myself that has taught me to have compassion and patience for others, because I am still going down some roads that I wish I could stop. It's not because of my addictive nature that I am an addict it is because I am an addict that I have an addictive nature. If it feels good, I'll do it. If it feels good and has a negative consequence, I may still do it. If it feels bad but I experience feelings because of it, I might do it. If my brain manufactures a chemical that makes me feel good or bad, if my organs manufacture a chemical that makes me feel good or bad, I'll feel it sometimes to my detriment. I think that it is important to talk about how addicts, while clean, sometimes feel their feelings to the point of producing adrenaline and endorphins or hormones in their body, like epinephrine, whether good or bad, that can ultimately cause us trouble.

Now I'm going to talk about some things that may be un-comfortable, if I haven't already. I have been addicted to porn for as long as I can remember, since the first time I saw it. I stop using porn when I am in a relationship but I always return to it. I hate this about myself. Using porn while in relationships, you're damn right, has caused me issues. Using porn while single has kept me single and unable in many ways to move on to my next relationship. Only one of my live-in girlfriends ever really suggested that I was looking at porn, and that was Jamie. At the time, I was using movie sites to watch movies, not to watch porn and Jamie came home one day and saw a pop-up from one of those movie sites which was a porn site advertisement and she called me very distressed and angry and said, "Pack your shit and get out." I was floored. She ultimately left me anyway but she was ready to leave me then. In every relationship I've ever been in, I don't think I have ever gone more than six months without looking at porn. It is by far my greatest addiction that I struggle with more than anything else.

Here's the scary part of porn, it keeps us alone. That's where most of us watch it, when we're alone and no one else is around. And where does the disease want to get us? It wants to keep us alone. Maybe one day I will be able to finally stop. I stopped the drugs, but I have not been able to stop my addiction to porn for very long. They say if we work the steps on specific issues in our lives, that the steps can help us stop other addictions as well. That is probably where this addict is headed next, a full round of steps on my addiction to porn. Humans are naturally sexual. I have been over sexual and it has taken its toll. Part of me being single, when I have been single, could possibly be attributed to my porn habit. I feel like most healthy couples with a healthy sex life, do not watch porn. They have each other, they are not alone.

Instead of going out to meet people some nights, I will just come home and stare at my phone for hours, saying that I don't have time to meet people and yet I find myself losing hours and hours to my disease in its current manifestation. This is the truth and I do not want to hold back in this book in any way from you or make you think that I have it all figured out. I will never have it all figured out. I may always struggle with some kind of addiction for the rest of my life, but I never have to get clean again. I never have to get high again. Using other things like a drug instead of drugs, is in no way justified. If we as addicts, are using porn like a drug, it is not a justified behavior even though it is not a drug, it can be just another trap that brings us unnecessary pain and ruins us from being present in our current and intimate relationships. It can also affect us in other areas of our life.

I would like to now get back to epinephrine, otherwise known as adrenaline, as well as the hormones and endorphins that our body produces when we are experiencing pain, anger, joy, peace, serenity or any other emotion or experiences that bring them into our system. They themselves can all be addictive, even the endorphins and hormones that cause us to feel physically bad. We are still feeling something when we are feeling them. It's like my buddy Marshall in Denver says, "This is a disease of emotions.", and emotions bring about those endorphins and hormones. A disease of feelings if you will, this disease of addiction. As addicts, we get addicted to feelings. Feeling high, feeling up, feeling down, it doesn't matter, either way we can become addicted to feelings. Addicts are famous for trying to change the way they feel. I cannot change the fact that I am an addict and I can-not change any of my past (both clean & using). Sometimes I just need to feel whatever feelings come through me and al-low those feelings to run their course without trying to control them or use a distraction to avoid them or produce any other feelings unnecessarily. Instead of trying to change the way I feel, I need to feel the way I change.

I'm glad I got clean at 15. Thank You and Thank God
—R

ACKNOWLEDGMENTS

I would like to thank all of my friends in the fellowship that have become my new family since the day I got clean.

Thank you to all of you who believed in me and all of you who believe in each other.

Without belief we have nothing.

Belief can be our greatest power.

IN LOVING MEMORY OF ALL THE ADDICTS WHO HAVE DIED FROM THE HORRORS OF ACTIVE ADDICTION RIP

ABOUT THE AUTHOR

Ryan Boyd's resolve to lead a chemical-free lifestyle at age fifteen and begin a life of recovery has not prevented the difficulties, obstacles, or heartbreak one may face in life. However, for the last twenty-three years, his determination to stay clean has been the grounding force to strive for a lifestyle that fosters abundant love for others, honesty, and adventure. A true renaissance man of the modern era, Ryan enjoys traditional bowhunting and yoga in his free time, and is quite handy around the house. In efforts to give back to the twelve-step fellowship that has supported him through both joyful and challenging times, Ryan has humbly served at the local, state, and national levels. Ryan received his creative writing degree from Murray State University. Find out more about Ryan at www.cleanat15.com.